Film light

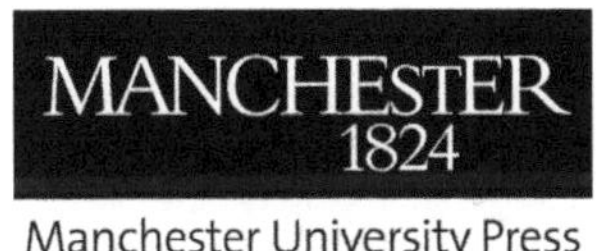

Manchester University Press

Film light

Meaning and emotion

Lara Thompson

Manchester University Press

Published by Manchester University Press
Altrincham Street, Manchester M1 7JA

www.manchesteruniversitypress.co.uk

British Library Cataloguing-in-Publication Data
A catalogue record for this book is available from the British Library

ISBN   978 0 7190 8634 2   paperback

This edition first published 2018

Typeset
by Carnegie Book Production, Lancaster
Printed by Lightning Source

Perhaps you'll think it strange that an invisible man should need light, desire light, love light. But maybe it is exactly because I *am* invisible. Light confirms my reality, gives birth to my form.

(Ralph Ellison, *Invisible Man*, 1952)

Contents

II The absence of light

Illustrations

Note: With the exception of Figure 32, all the images in this
book are screen grabs, reproduced under the Fair Dealing
guidelines relating to criticism and review, as suggested by the
Intellectual Property Office (published 12 June 2014).

Acknowledgements

This book would not have been completed without the help of a few steadfast and supportive individuals. I want to thank Matthew Frost at MUP for his unwavering faith in the work and for allowing me the space to get it right. Heartfelt thanks also go to Steven Peacock for his insightful and encouraging comments, removals and additions. Without the invaluable discussions and debates in seminars and out-of-hours with my colleagues, students and friends at Birkbeck College I would have missed the meaningful and emotive light in a number of films, so many thanks to everyone who offered suggestions. An early version of Chapter 5 was adapted from a section of my Ph.D. thesis and as such I am also indebted to my supervisor Laura Mulvey whose kind generosity, formidable cinematic knowledge and unshakeable support I would have been lost without. I am also eternally grateful to my fellow Ph.D. candidate and long-time friend Marlène Monteiro for her time-consuming, accurate and much appreciated translation work.

Finally, and most importantly, I would like to thank Charlie, Larry and Jeanette for motivation, will power and patience respectively and for love all round.

This book is dedicated to Luca – bringer of light.

Introduction

Light is at once universal and elusive.

(Paul Hills, *The Light of Early Italian Painting*, 1987)

To choose to talk about light in cinema is to choose the evidence, with its traps.

(Jacques Aumont, *L'attrait de la lumière*, 2010)

Light is cinema's most essential quality. Illumination is not only the means through which the image is created, it is also the material, either natural or projected, through which the image is made visible. As Mike O'Pray has noted, film and photography use light as both agency and object.[1] Fundamentally, then, films *are* light. And yet, perhaps as a result of light's all-encompassing nature, across the history of narrative film theory and criticism, its aesthetic attributes, its visual impact and emotional affect has thus far been marginalised, mentioned only in biographies of cinematographers or in relation to practical techniques, confined to debates around certain film cycles such as film noir, or amalgamated into more general discussions concerning *mise-en-scène*. Although a number of books touch on lighting aesthetics, from Arnheim's descriptions of the film artist's power to induce emotion according to where he places his lamps in *Film as Art*, to Schivelbusch's notion of a viewer hypnotically submerged in flame-like screen light in *Disenchanted Night*, to O'Pray's investigations into light's sculptural, modelling capacities in *Film, Form and Phantasy*, at the time of writing only a single recent monograph – Jacques Aumont's small, philosophical, essential *L'attrait de la lumière* concentrates entirely on the seductive visual power of cinematic light.[2] The pervasive, nebulous nature of illumination in the cinema makes it a problematic unifying subject. It is at once ubiquitous and difficult to grasp, flickering across the faces of every character on the screen and spectator in the audience, pushing into the corners of every shot, infiltrating the image on every level.

While all films need light as a means of vision so that the spectator can literally see the actors, sets and scenes, this book is concerned with the use of light as an artistic narrative tool that creates meaning. It focuses on over fifty films in which light has transcended its diffuse functional boundaries and been elevated to a position of narrative and emotional importance, transforming it from an inconspicuous element of film style to an expressive and essential component, emphasising light's status as 'a representational element in its own right, along with figures and objects'.[3] The films are primarily, but not exclusively, drawn from the dominant modes of narrative cinema, the canon, as well as the popular: the aim is to suggest a means of navigating the use and meaning of light from within the known histories of the moving image, from cinema's earliest moments to its most recent digital manifestations. It seeks to use films that are familiar and readily available, so that the reader may revisit, reimagine and actively participate in the study of film light.

Since the aesthetic study of illumination is relatively uncharted, especially within narrative cinema, it seemed pertinent for an introductory study such as this to return to cinema classics and frequently negotiated favourites including *Nosferatu* (*Nosferatu, eine Symphonie des Grauens*, Murnau, 1922), *The Third Man* (Reed, 1949) and *Breathless* (*À bout de souffle*, Godard, 1960) as a means of grounding the arguments and analyses within cinematic history and of highlighting the rich textural qualities of these films that allow multivalent readings and varied perspectives. Simply put, the canon is the most logical place to start. This is not to say that a study of light's aesthetic import in avant-garde and experimental cinema is not needed, but rather that since much of the work on alternative filmmakers and film artists from Stan Brakhage and Holis Frampton to Maya Deren and Lis Rhodes, or more recently the work of Tacita Dean and Ben Rivers attests, like the artists themselves, writers in this field have always been sensitive to the lyrical importance of illumination, to the link between cinematic ontology and its visual affect(s). It is narrative cinema in which light has hitherto been ignored. At the same time, the inclusion of more recent films such as *Batman Begins* (Nolan, 2005) and *A Single Man* (Ford, 2009), bring the work up to date to push past the canon, extending the field of study towards the popular and the critically contentious. The use of these films notes light's visual and emotive importance to both the general viewer and the populist filmmaker. The films I refer to, while particular in their use of light, are also often used to illustrate a trend. While they are examples that can stand in for any number of films that use light in similar ways, they are also exemplary and significant in their use of light, earning their place in the canon and in the popular imagination, precisely because they use varying shades and swathes of light at key moments not only as the agent and object of their vision, but as one of the defining methods of their emotive narrative exposition.

Across all the chapters, as the book's title implies, this work is particularly interested in the way filmmakers have harnessed light's expressive qualities in an attempt to make both the visual experience evoke wider narrative information (for the aesthetic decisions to connote meaning) and to induce or heighten emotional responses in the spectator. This is not to say that the book is concerned with emotion or meaning as subject matter, with the various theoretical stances attached to the viable and engaging work on emotion in film studies seen in cognitive film theory and the work of Murray Smith, Ed Tan and Cynthia Freeland, or to the recent widespread attention devoted to 'affect' or the 'haptic' in film studies.[4] Rather, this book is engaged in the project of examining the visible, textual connections between aesthetic lighting decisions and an intended spectatorial response, regardless of whether that response is actually experienced. It is about the way certain instances of illumination and darkness seem to encourage particular emotional experiences and narrative associations. To borrow Smith's term, in this context, the 'structure of sympathy' emerges as much from the kind of light that strikes a character's face as it does from the extent to which we engage with their words and actions.[5] This is not emotion and meaning as theory, but as illuminated stylistic endeavour.

In order to confront the difficulty of analysing such an essential but amorphous subject across the history of cinema, taking in multiple modes, genres and meanings, it has been necessary to impose a structure. As such this book maintains a basic opposition between illumination and darkness. The dialectic reinforces the sense that in the cinema the absence of light is as significant as its presence: film can only be experienced through the interplay between what is lit and what is not. The division of this book into two sections – Part I 'The presence of light' and Part II 'The absence of light' – notes a visual and emotional distinction as opposed to an oppositional critical stance, highlighting the fundamental visual nature of cinematic light as a dualistic sculpting tool, its ability to create areas on the screen that are not only illuminated, but that also languish in shadow, its capacity to both prioritise and conceal people and spaces. While intense light dominates attention, darkness lingers in stark silhouettes, black doorways and moody blue twilight. Both states are equally significant in the history of cinema. While every chapter necessarily engages with both light and dark, this relationship offers a way of engaging with the fundamental elements of cinematic illumination: in Part I, how people, and particularly faces, are illuminated; how architecture sculpts natural illumination; how the imaginary is created with light, as well as suggestions regarding the various meanings associated with these types of illumination. Only then are we able to concentrate on what happens when light leaves the screen, when it wanes or disappears, focusing on the creation of suspense, the partial illumination used in contemporary representations of history, and twilight cinematic states. These darker chapters of Part II do not oppose, but rather work in dialogue with the first brightly lit Part I. Each one continues to engage with notions of characterisation, environment and artifice, while expanding the study to include a light-oriented focus on our understanding of film genre and relationship with film history. Across all these chapters themes of realism, illusion and spectacle emerge, repeat and are reinforced.

At the same time, this book attempts to be sensitive to the complex, shifting and multifarious nature of cinematic light, emphasising its varied tones and intensities, its constant pliability, its suggestive and associative uses. While light is either visible or missing, shadows and spotlights, electric illumination and the lyricism of cinematic dawns and dusks all suggest that presence is itself *heightened* by absence, while the reverse is also the case. In between the two poles of a total white-out and a pitch-black void, innumerable combinations of light and shade encourage varied, yet specific readings. Stylistically recalling the expressive criticism of writers such as Andrew Klevan, Steven Peacock, George Toles and William Rothman, this book is also interested in the synthetic unity of film's components of style heralded by V. F. Perkins in *Film as Film* (1970). As such, each of the chapters notes light's intersection with other areas of film form to produce and suggest meaning – with set design, gesture, camera movement, costume, monochrome tones and coloured hues – while emphasising the notion that light also produces its own distinct affects: if lit in different ways an empty room can evoke varying atmospheres, temporalities and emotions from the comforting golden sunlight of a day's end, to the harsh blue-white hues of eerie science fiction. Although difficult to define, cinematic light *can* be grouped into areas of meaning, examined in associated patterns.

Chapter 1 'Identity' looks at how the face and the body have been lit, from the development of functional lighting to the Hollywood Studio 'star close-up' and the way in which faces and bodies are fetishised by light into objects of sympathy, desire, revelation and individuality. Films in this chapter include *La passion de Jeanne d'Arc* (*The Passion of Joan of Arc*, Dreyer, 1928), *Blonde Venus* (Sternberg, 1932), *Gentlemen Prefer Blondes* (Hawks, 1953), *The Third Man, Apocalypse Now* (Coppola, 1979) and *Morvern Callar* (Ramsay, 2002). It argues that dramatic lighting tells the spectator where to look and who to look at, it isolates the face and body, attracting the gaze and encouraging an emotional attachment to protagonists whose identities are formed through moments of expressive lighting.

Chapter 2 'Authenticity' focuses on the use of naturalistic daylight to provide authentic, energetic experiences that use verité aesthetics to create 'modern' characters, from Italian neo-realism to the *nouvelle vague*, from British kitchen-sink dramas to Dogme 95. Films include *Bicycle Thieves* (*Ladri di biciclette*, De Sica, 1948), *Breathless, A Taste of Honey* (Richardson, 1961) and *The Celebration* (*Festen*, Vinterberg, 1998). This chapter suggests that 'natural' light in the cinema is as constructed as artificial studio lighting and thus must be understood as a similar form of cinematic 'spectacle'.

Chapter 3 'The imaginary' examines the ways in which light has been used expressively to create magical alternative worlds and authenticate fantasy spaces, from *Metropolis* (Lang, 1927) to *An American in Paris* (Minnelli, 1951) to *Close Encounters of the Third Kind* (Spielberg, 1977) and *Three Colours: Blue* (*Trois couleurs: bleu*, Kieslowśki, 1993). In these films light is the medium through which the imaginary is realised, it verifies computer-generated landscapes and marks out alien races as 'other', while at the same time highlighting more recognisable environments as internal character fantasies.

Part II 'The absence of light', focuses on dark, interstitial and existential illumination. Chapter 4 'Mystery' looks at chiaroscuro and expressive lighting techniques across a range of film genres that limit the use of light to create suspense, threatening atmospheres and ambivalent protagonists. Films include *Nosferatu, Once Upon a Time in the West* (*C'era una volt ail West*, Leone, 1968), *Blue Velvet* (Lynch, 1986) and *Batman Begins*. Here shadows, tunnels and hiding places both protect and threaten, putting illuminated existence under threat, encouraging spectatorial anxiety or fear, and harbouring confused, morally ambiguous characters who at once seek out, yet remain afraid of, the dark.

Chapter 5 'The past' argues that when reconstructing history, films often reproduce the lighting styles and techniques of previous eras in order to substantiate their versions of the past, especially with regard to film noir lighting aesthetics. Here the past is dimly lit, a gloomy, almost unknowable shadow of a memory that is fading, while conversely stark monochrome reduces light to certainties, offering up distinct, oppositional myths of the past. In this chapter, films including *Raging Bull* (Scorsese, 1980), *The Man Who Wasn't There* (Coen, 2001), *Sin City* (Miller and Rodriguez, 2005) and *A Single Man* will be examined to show how black and white, subdued or darkly coloured lighting is used to historicise character and place, creating a muted, photographically familiar, self-referential film world.

Finally, Chapter 6 'The magic hour' focuses on moments of twilight in cinema as an interstitial state between waking and dreaming akin to the cinematic experience itself. It shows how digital technological developments are allowing films to depict twilight states with greater ease, where light (and character identity) is always dying but never dead, and where waxing or waning illumination indicates both alternative, interior selves and dream-like dislocations from reality. Films include *La notte* (*The Night*, Antonioni, 1961), *The Birds* (Hitchcock, 1963), *Fight Club* (Fincher, 1999) and *Donnie Darko* (Kelly, 2001). Part II of the book does not oppose, but rather works in dialogue with Part I. Each chapter continues to engage with ideas of characterisation, environment and artifice.

While some films generally lean towards one style of lighting, at the same time they all use different kinds of lighting at various times, often in contradictory ways. In order to express the breadth of light used and the range of its emotive affect, multiple scenes illustrate the discussion throughout. In each chapter, close light readings allow significant relationships between films that would not normally be placed together to surface, in turn illuminating them in new ways outside of their traditional generic positions. Key instants of arresting expressive light, including the moment Harry (Orson Welles) runs down dark tunnels dripping with torchlight at the end of *The Third Man*, Julie's expressive coloured waves of despair in *Three Colours: Blue*, and the kaleidoscopic space-blasts of transcendental split-scan technology in *2001: A Space Odyssey* (Kubrick, 1968), are discussed a number of times, re-examining their use of light to suggest various meanings. As Patrick Keating notes below, as context shifts, so too does our interpretation of a film's lighting style:

> We should resist the temptation to assign a fixed meaning to any one lighting technique. The same device can appear in dozens of different conventions, as in the following options: When you are photographing a night exterior, consider low-key lighting. When you are photographing a male character actor, consider low-key lighting. When you are photographing a crime scene, consider low-key lighting. The fact that low-key lighting can serve in multiple conventions means that its own significance is not fixed. Low-key lighting does not mean 'sinister' lighting, and backlighting does not mean 'angelic' lighting. Just as we need context to understand the meaning of a word, we need context to understand the meaning of a lighting technique.[6]

This book is neither a technical manual on lighting technology, nor is it a history of lighting in the cinema. Instead, using detailed

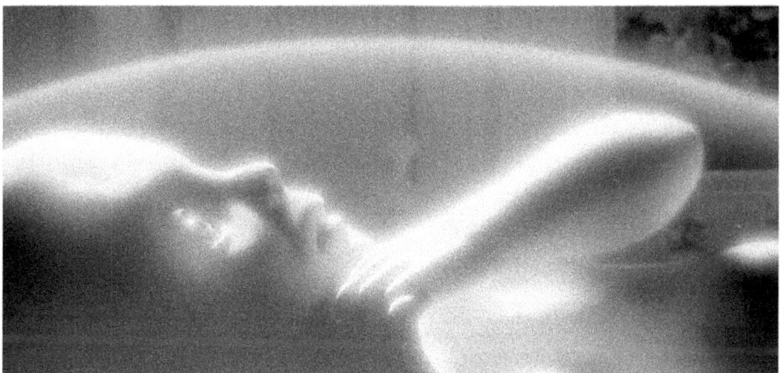

1   *2001: A Space Odyssey*. Kubrick's luminous Star Child

textual analysis to re-evaluate a broad range of well-known films, it attempts to show how an understanding of the ways in which light has been used aesthetically can transform our understanding and appreciation of cinema's emotive attractions. Ultimately it argues that as the screen shimmers and shifts, our relationship with film light and its meaning is similarly transformative and complex, encouraging us to variously and vicariously feel, remember, marvel and witness. While light reveals character identity and expresses emotional experience, it also, in its transformation of time and space, delays and absorbs the viewer formally, forging heightened connections between spectator, protagonist and image. Light's atmospheric luminosity seduces the eye, and in turn encourages a kind of concentrated, emotive and valued cinematic gaze. Through a discussion of light, cinema begins to reveal itself: not just the angles of its sets, the emotions of its characters or the intensity of its atmospheres, but its apparatus and ontology, its manipulation of environment and time. This book is not intended as the last word on the aesthetics of cinematic illumination, but rather, it is hoped, one of the first – an initial tentative gesture towards the light. As Aumont suggests at the end of *L'attrait de la lumière*: '[T]here is no limit to the expressive ambition that one can have in cinema about and thanks to light.'[7]

Notes

1 M. O'Pray, *Film, Form and Phantasy: Adrian Stokes and Film Aesthetics* (New York: Palgrave Macmillan, 2004), p. 196.
2 See R. Arnheim, *Film as Art* (London: University of California Press, 1933/1957), pp. 66–7; W. Schivelbusch, *Disenchanted Night: The Industrialization of Light in the Nineteenth Century* (Berkeley, Los Angeles and London: University of California Press, 1988), pp. 220–1.
3 O'Pray, *Film, Form and Phantasy*, p. 198.
4 See M. Smith, *Engaging Characters: Fiction, Emotion and the Cinema* (New York: Oxford University Press, 1995); E. Tan, *Emotion and the Structure of Narrative Film: Film as an Emotion Machine* (London: Routledge, 1995); L. Podalsky, *The Politics of Affect and Emotion in Latin American Cinema* (New York: Palgrave Macmillan, 2011); C. Plantinga and G. M. Smith, *Passionate Views: Film, Cognition and Emotion* (Baltimore: John Hopkins University Press, 1999); J. Halley and P. Ticineto Clough, *The Affective Turn: Theorizing the Social* (Durham, NC: Duke University Press, 2007).
5 See Smith, *Engaging Characters*, pp. 4–5.
6 P. Keating, *Hollywood Lighting from the Silent Era to Film Noir* (New York: Columbia University Press, 2010), p. 2
7 Jacques Aumont, *L'attrait de la lumière* (Crisnée: Éditions Yellow Now, 2010), p. 77.

1   The presence of light

1 Identity

> The identity of the image and movement stems from the identity of matter and light.
>
> > (Gilles Deleuze, *The Movement Image*, 1983/86)

> Step out in the light and let's have a look at ya.
>
> > (Holly Martin (Joseph Cotten) to Harry Lime
> > (Orson Welles), *The Third Man*)

Light is both the character and the identity of the projected image. Without light the screen world would not exist: no sets, no props, no actors; no love affairs, no adventures, no heroes. There would be nothing to see and no one to look at. The film that flew through the projector would remain transparent, digital sensors would lie dormant; a white square would not appear on a blank wall in a darkened room. Light is the substance out of which the image is made as well as the reason we can see what the image captures. In those early years of the medium when workers left factories and trains entered stations, as filmmakers experimented with film stock and lenses and narrative arcs, their first and overriding preoccupation was how to get enough light into their cameras so that what they filmed could be seen and preserved. This need to harness illumination in specific strengths and textures drove almost every early production-based decision, from the necessity of shooting outdoors under bright day-time skies, to the move into glass studios where light could be prolonged and redirected, to the incorporation of electric arc lights and three-point studio lighting. Each technological advance harnessed more (intense/malleable/diffuse) light for the camera to consume and project so that objects, people and scenes could be illuminated and visualised in new, more realistic or more expressive ways.

At the same time, light in the cinema is far more than a practical necessity. As much as light brings both the projected image and the subject of the projection into existence, it also indicates to the spectator where to look, who to look at and how to feel. A directional, bright or dramatic light entices and seduces the eye. It draws the gaze, centralising the 'look' at the brightest point on the screen, focusing attention on those parts of the image that the filmmaker deems important. In a similar way to a flashbulb going off in the dark, or a beam of torchlight on a black night, the eye clings to intense light in cinema, a primitive throwback, perhaps, to a period in human evolution during which darkness meant the danger of the unknown world outside the cave and light was connected to the safety of knowledge and understanding beside the fire. This dialectic between positive illumination and negative darkness, in a continuation of religious symbolism and art practice, has been reinforced throughout cinematic history. It is the quality of light, its presence or absence, its strength or direction, that frequently marks the aesthetic and atmospheric difference between a romance or a horror, a hero or a villain, a virgin or a vamp. When experimentation, deviation, or reversal occurs, the oppositional duality remains. Catherine Tramell's stark whiteness in *Basic Instinct* (Paul Verhoeven, 1992) cloaks her dark interior. In *Donnie Darko* (Richard Kelly, 2001) the protagonist's interstitial identity as a teenager who may or may not be dead is visible in the indeterminate twilight that surrounds him. In each case, the identity of the image itself, along with the identity of the character on-screen, is in part communicated through light and shadow.

The human face with its vital expressivity and immediate capacity for identification has become one of the primary subjects of dramatic light in the cinema. An illuminated facial close-up brings the person in the light into being. We come to know characters, to love their quirks and personalities, their pouts and winks, to sympathise, loathe or desire them through the way their features are lit up on the screen. As Richard Dyer has noted, the cinema has privileged the face, in particular the white face, not least because of its supposed capacity to reflect light and thus attract the gaze of the viewer.[1] When a person's face reflects the light in an aesthetically pleasing way, they are often described as 'photogenic', a quality many stars have of looking more attractive once filmed or photographed. Three-point studio lighting enhanced this effect. The combination of a primary *key* light, a softer *fill* light and *backlighting* divorced the actor from their environment and pushed them out, drawing them closer to those watching on the other side of the screen. Blonde haloes, dramatic make-up, sculpted cheekbones, bright eyes beneath the darkened tip of a black hat: all service the light to help make a star shine. The particularities of facial illumination offer a direct example of the way lighting highlights expression in order to communicate and facilitate emotion. In the films discussed in this chapter, light both forms and compliments character identity: the protagonist's narrative arc is mapped via shifting lighting techniques that work as an indication to the spectator of the emotional thrust of any given scene. Variations in the tone, contrast or intensity of lighting aim to induce sympathy, adoration or identification. Ultimately, the desire to exist on-screen, to be a star, or to love one, is driven by the relationship between an actor's face and the light that makes their immortality possible.

Sympathy

Direct unflinching illumination marks out protagonists and encourages sympathetic alignment. Lighting denotes the hierarchy of our attachment to the characters on the screen. In *La passion de Jeanne d'Arc* (Carl Theodor Dreyer, 1928) lighting combines with the close-up and Maria Falconetti's extraordinary performance to project an arresting vision of the French martyr infused with compassion and sorrow. The film evokes the pain of human sacrifice via aesthetic experimentation. Through stark lighting and tight framing Dreyer divorces Jeanne's face from her body, transforming her into an intensely sympathetic cinematic fetish; her devastated features fill the screen forging an enduring emblem of pure emotional force.

At the start of the film the camera is overhead as Jeanne moves forward in chains to swear on the Bible. White walls behind her frame a single latticed window, while the Bible itself is padlocked, emphasising the inevitability of her fate. Everything in the frame has been stripped back: a barely there set, muted robes and the absence of dramatic make-up reflect the rigid religious austerity that pervades the proceedings. Jeanne looks petrified as she takes the stand before the Judge. Her hair is short and dark; it shines in the glossy light. Her eyes are wide with large circles of bright illumination glinting off their wet surface like those of a wild animal caught in the headlights of a speeding car. The dark iris that circles the field of vision, as it does in many films from this era, condenses and intensifies the action within, creating a halo of shading around the edges of the screen that functions like a second frame to concentrate the gaze. As the judge speaks, the light throbs around him; grey edges shrink and retract like an elastic band of blackness tightening and expanding, throttling the frame. Just as Jeanne's world has been reduced to the white walls of her judgment room and cell, so too has the second shadow-frame squeezed and heightened the action mirroring her entrapment. Jeanne's face, along with those of the judges

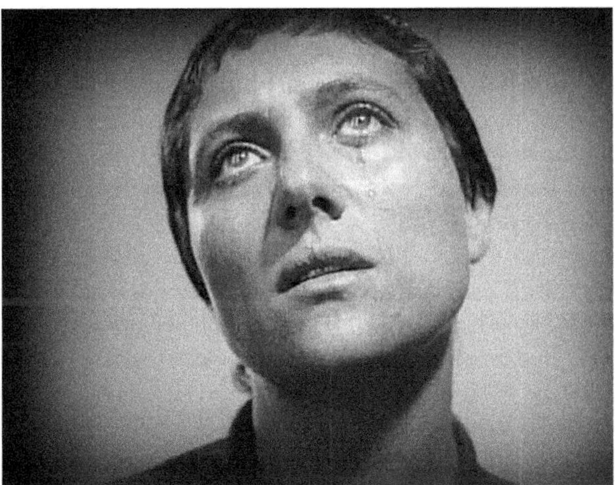

2 *The Passion of Joan of Arc/La passion de Jeanne d'Arc.* Tears catch the light on Jeanne's (Maria Falconetti) devastated face

and priests that surround her, floats in suffocating proximity to the screen: she cannot escape her destiny, just as the spectator is unable to escape this vision of her suffering. We can look at almost nothing and no one else; the intent of the lighting and framing is clear. All that matters is this face and humanity's reflective potential to shine forth from it.

Although the harsh frontal lighting illuminates everyone similarly, it also distinguishes the young Jeanne from those who sit in ageing male judgment around her; its stark intensity makes shadows and gullies out of the wrinkles on her accuser's faces, further contorting their sneers and aggression. Jeanne's plain, muted surroundings echo her white-grey skin, so that only the shadows cast by light falling on her features makes them stand out; her eyes, nose and lips rise out of the blankness as though she has been moulded out of putty-coloured clay. Here the particular impact of the dimensions of an actress's face and the effect of certain styles of lighting on the construction of the codes of sympathy and desire can be seen. The shape of Falconetti's face is formed in such a way – a high forehead, large eyes, soft round contours, lack of aggressive definition – so that light hits almost every part of it evenly. The sculptural cheekbones of Garbo and Dietrich that cast overt shadows of statuesque desire are absent, as is the masque-like make-up of Monroe that pushes out ruby lips and emphasises seductive kohl-lined eyes. In *Jeanne d'Arc* Falconetti's face is unadorned, modern and iconic. The lack of dramatic make-up imbues the film with emotional realism. Her eyes are open wounds embedded in a stark face of naked simplicity upon which light is given free-reign to roam, pricking spectatorial reaction to the core.

Dreyer's excessive use of eye light is crucial to the emotional force of the film. Placed on the same level as an actor's eyes and benefiting from their naturally reflective wetness, eye light is simply defined by cinematographer John Alton as a light that is 'used to brighten up the eyes of individuals'.[2] As is so often the case with discussions of lighting in the cinema, the emotional and aesthetic attributes of eye light as a significant tool of expression are rarely discussed. Eye light adds spirit, intensity and life to an actor's performance. Just as it is harder to connect in conversation to a person whose eyes are concealed (by sunglasses for example) the affect of the illuminated eye encourages connection, empathy, realism. On-screen it is one of the reasons the spectator becomes emotionally involved in the inner life of a character. It helps to form sympathy and allegiances across cinematic space, drawing us towards the performer, while holding the potential to transform otherwise lacklustre performances into believable human experience. Of all the characters' eyes in Dreyer's film, it is Jeanne's, stretched taught in fear and despair, which are the largest, and thus the eye light that they capture and project is the brightest. In comparison to the men in the room, whose eyes are either hidden in the shadows and folds of age where light cannot penetrate, or pierced with cold flecks that are suggestive of anger or indifference, Jeanne's doe eyes constantly soak up eye light and bounce it back at the lens. Allusions to wide-eyed innocence abound. The light that shines off the surface of her eyes heightens the sense that she is desperate to both save and be saved. At times the eye light becomes so bright and the camera moves so close that Dreyer's constructed world of lamps and sets becomes momentarily visible within Jeanne's own stricken gaze, simultaneously shattering the cinematic illusion and grounding Falconetti's emotional performance in the real world.

Jeanne breaks down completely when the judge asks who taught her the Lord's Prayer. As she replies 'Ma mère' she becomes more and more distressed – every lip quiver, every sob, every signifier of suffering is captured in extreme close-up beneath unwavering light until a single tear rolls down her face like a tiny luminescent ball. It is a moment that recalls the evocative connection between water, light and lyricism. As Jeanne cries more intensely, the light captures the way her tears leave silver-grey tracks in her pale make-up. The more her eyes fill, the more they well up with light and overflow; here intensifying illumination becomes directly linked to increasing emotion. When her eyes close momentarily, we, like Jeanne, experience relief because her pool-like eyes, the signifiers of her sorrow, have been briefly hidden from view.

On the rare occasions when Dreyer's camera moves away from intimate facial close-ups, light continues to induce emotion and evoke associative meaning within the frame. After her judgment has been read, in utter despair, Jeanne is taken to her cell. Sitting on the edge of her bed, struggling to breathe through the pain and her tears, with death so close at hand, she becomes hysterical. Hands rake over her once-controlled face and she writhes in agony as though she has lost her mind. Suddenly, she sees something out of the corner of her eye and pauses, momentarily enraptured. The film cuts to the floor of her cell, and there, formed by the light cast between the bars of her prison window, is the shadow of a cross. Jeanne interprets this image of light as a sign from God. She becomes calm, her strength and hope is restored and for the first time in the film she smiles. Light renews her strength.

While Jeanne's fortitude remains intact, her respite from the pain of judgment is brief. At the end of the film, after recanting her admission of guilt, she is tied to the stake. Once lit, the smoke from the raging fire at her feet consumes both Jeanne and the frame, muting the world in shifting grey light, concealing the horror from view. As she burns, the crowd riots. Through the smoke and flames, the priests and judges look on as her burnt body transforms into a black shadow in the midst of the fire. Light in its purest form destroys the face it once encouraged us to love. Sorrow overwhelms. An intertitle reads: 'The flames sheltered Jeanne's soul as it rose to heaven.' Here the shifting firelight becomes representative of both the momentary sorrow of death and the everlasting promise of salvation. In a reversal of the light–dark dichotomy, the film suggests Jeanne's soul resides in shadow form, eternally fixed like a dark symbol of hope amidst the bright flames of religious condemnation.

Desire

Where stark lighting on a wide-eyed unadorned face turns Falconetti into an icon of sympathetic despair, the glossy Hollywood lustre of 'movie lighting' on dramatic features enables certain actors to project epic star appeal. Simplistically defined as the three-point studio lighting system of *key*, *fill* and *backlighting* developed in the 1920s and used (along with various additional light sources) throughout mainstream cinematic history, movie lighting, according to Richard Dyer, guarantees that 'what is important in a shot is clearly visible to the audience'.[3] Movie lighting prioritises and isolates certain areas of the frame (most frequently actors' faces) over others. With its capacity to separate while sculpting in three dimensions, it draws out objects and characters from their backgrounds, guiding the gaze. Dyer argues that this kind of film lighting frequently prioritises the face, particularly the white female face with its capacity for excessive reflection, over everything else in the frame. Because of its ability to elevate and exaggerate, as Dyer notes, '"movie lighting" valorises the notion of the unique and special character of the individual, of the individuality of the individual'.[4] In combination with a particular smile or cheekbone, movie lighting differentiates certain actors from their peers, elevating their presence on-screen, encouraging the spectator's desire. In short, this kind of illumination creates stars.

Movie lighting marks out Marlene Dietrich and Marilyn Monroe as special in two films with titles that draw attention to their iconic hair colour: *Blonde Venus* (Joseph von Sternberg, 1932) and *Gentlemen Prefer Blondes* (Howard Hawks, 1953). Each woman has an intimate relationship with film light: it caresses them, highlighting those parts of their features and figures that mark them out as desirable individual stars. On-screen, along with the costumes and blonde hair that adorn them, the two women entice, reflect and refract the light. At the same time, the swooping arc of each character's narrative trajectory – of Helen Faraday (Dietrich) and Lorelei Lee (Monroe) – from contented status quo through action and despair to redemption, is marked by the shifting quality of film light as it projects onto them and is reflected through the screen. In each film Dietrich and Monroe play showgirls who perform song and dance numbers on stage at pivotal narrative moments. This device, much used in the classical Hollywood musical, enables the quality and intensity of the light that shines upon them to transform and escalate at key emotional points without breaking away from the logical flow of the film's diegesis.

When Ned Faraday stumbles across his future wife Helen bathing with other chorus girls in a sun-dappled pool in the opening scene of *Blonde Venus* he is arrested not by her naked body, but by her striking face. While the tantalising pale nudity of the other women is just visible beneath the shifting surface of the water, their faces remain anonymous, their identities unknown. Helen swims to the fore, jutting her head and shoulders through the undergrowth to ask the men to leave. Soft backlighting glints in her hair, fine eyebrows trail off into alabaster skin, heavy-lidded eyes frown above sculpted cheekbones, full lips part: she speaks. The combination of Dietrich's dramatic face with the diffuse lighting that softens it creates a heady moment pregnant with desire. This luminous opening, and Ned's reluctance to leave, draws immediate attention to Helen's dangerously irresistible qualities, marking the beginning of her magnetic relationship with light.

Dietrich's star persona along with Helen's emotional experience and our level of spectatorial attachment to her, continue to be communicated throughout the film by the wax and wane of von Sternberg's lyrical lighting techniques. Now married, Ned and Helen tuck up their son Johnny in bed and retell the story of their first meeting by the pool in Germany. Shot in medium close-up Helen sits to the left of Johnny's crib while Ned stands on the right. Helen is drenched in slanting bright light that pours in from the left-hand side of the frame. Due to its origin and direction, the light hits her first, bouncing off white shirt-clad shoulders and glistening blonde hair, before illuminating Johnny in his crib and finally Ned on the other side. As the light travels across each character it weakens so that the hierarchy of spectatorial interest is mapped in illumination. Ned and Johnny bask in Helen's glow.

This strong angelic light that at once emanates from and envelopes Helen continues throughout the first section of the film reaching an apex of luminosity during her first stage performance. In need of money to fund her husband's experimental treatment Helen returns to singing. In the casting office her specialness is indicated by the brightness of the light that hits her face, leaving the other girls in the dark: it is no surprise when she is selected. Preparing in the club before her performance, Helen's narrative superiority to the other singer, brunette Taxi Belle Hooper (Rita La Roy), is once more visible

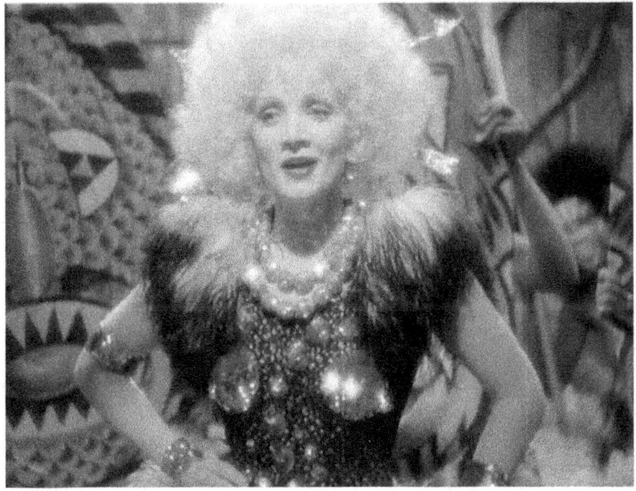

3   *Blonde Venus*. Helen's (Marlene Dietrich) glittering corset

via the intensified strength of her facial illumination. Further juxtaposition continues onstage when Helen emerges from a black gorilla costume to sing a lusty voodoo song. Behind her the comparison is drawn against the young black women with giant afro wigs who dance unnoticed in the gloom. In the audience Nick Townsend (Gary Grant) watches enthralled as Helen removes the gorilla's head and replaces it with an enormous fluffy blonde wig. As Dietrich slides out of the rest of her costume, revealing a tight-fitting bodice encrusted with hundreds of sparkling diamonds, she reaches the pinnacle of her visual power as a star. Nick gazes up adoringly from below, his eyes sparkling in the glow cast from her pulsating breast plate; every part of her blasts light and sensuality into the audience and through the screen as his desire for her becomes our own.

In its lighting style, use of costume and emotive intent, Dietrich's first number in *Blonde Venus* anticipates Monroe's sparkling opening performance of 'Two Little Girls from Little

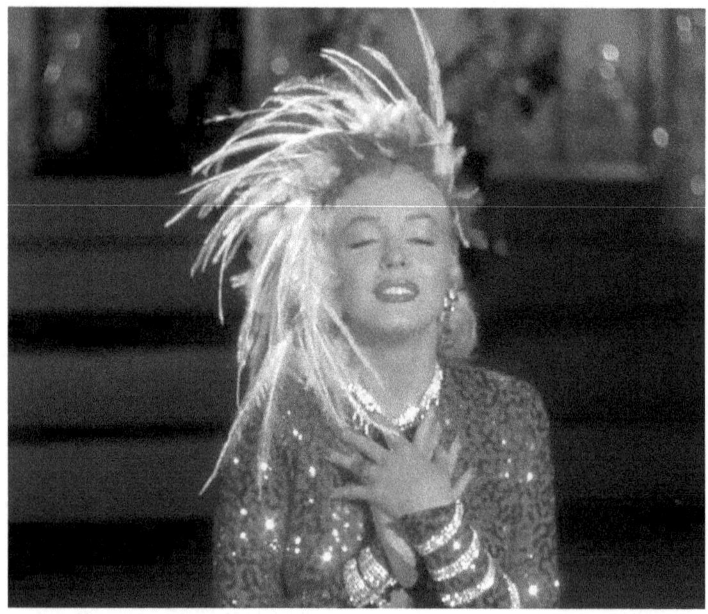

4 *Gentlemen Prefer Blondes*. Diamonds sparkle on Lorelei's (Marilyn Monroe) jewel-encrusted gown

Rock' in *Gentlemen Prefer Blondes*. Here vibrant Technicolor hues and Monroe's sensual diamond-encrusted bright red dress add to the sexual electricity of the act. Although at the time of filming Jane Russell was arguably the bigger star, in this number Monroe literally steals the limelight. Even though they wear identical outfits and dance in unison, Monroe's blonde hair, ice-white smile and milky make-up (two or three shades lighter than Russell's) ensures she is more reflective, encouraging greater attention and elevating her star power. Light clings to Monroe's face, shining off her bright red lips, pushing them towards the spectator in a glossy trade-mark pout. Just as Helen's electrified torso encouraged the desiring glance of Nick in the audience, so too does Lorelei's sparkling costume captivate Gus's (Tommy Noonan) gaze. In each case it is diamonds, and their association with wealth, luxury and illumination that cling to these women. As much as they make her shine, Lorelei's obsession with diamonds – her superficial desire to sparkle and appear rich – leads to her downfall. After she convinces Piggy (Charles Coburn) to give her his wife's diamond tiara, his wife reports it stolen causing Lorelei and Dorothy to be kicked out of their hotel in Paris. Homeless, they stop in a café and sing 'When Love Goes Wrong, Nothing Goes Right'. Again, although they are dressed similarly, certain aspects of Lorelei's costume – her wide, white, open collar, her white gloves, her blonde hair under a dark hat – mean that she attracts and projects the light more efficiently than Dorothy. Costume combines with Monroe's physical attributes and the light cast upon them, to amplify her star status and reflect narrative shifts in her character's fortunes.

In a similar way, in *Blonde Venus*, as much as light illuminated Helen's rise, its absence marks her fall. After Ned returns from Europe a cured man, he discovers Helen's affair with Nick and forbids her from ever seeing Johnny again. She goes on the run with Johnny, travelling from club to club singing under various aliases while Ned tries to track her down with the help of the police. Light leaves her by degrees. At first, on stage, the diamonds on her costume that made her shine slip from her torso to her thigh leaving muted swathes of black velvet around her face that absorb the light. When Ned finally catches up with Helen and takes Johnny away, she drinks too much and descends into depression dressed only in blacks and greys, while wearing a battered hat that blocks most of the light from her face. Even her blonde hair has lost its halo and shine.

After reaching rock bottom in a women's refuge, Helen vows to sleep in a better bed and her rebirth as a shining star begins. Like Lorelei, she goes to Paris, her successful re-entry into the world of entertaining announced by the now ubiquitous cliché of her name repeated on the screen in flashing lights. On stage her luminosity returns. In a masculine white tuxedo accessorised with glittering diamonds on its lapel, she is once more framed with illumination. Around her the other girls dressed in black with nets over their faces cease to exist. This technique of cladding the faces of backing dancers in black veils so that they merge into the background is also used when Lorelei sings 'Diamonds are a Girl's Best Friend' towards the end of *Gentlemen Prefer Blondes*. As the number begins, dancers dressed in black appear tethered to a giant black candelabra spinning in the middle of the stage. The suggestion that women on-screen are both agents of and slaves to the light is reinforced. A number of other dancers swathed in candy-pink ruffles run onto the stage. Each of them wears a black net veil, concealing their faces from view. When Lorelei, also dressed in fuchsia, sings next to them, in comparison the veiled girls look like anonymous shadows and Monroe with her blonde hair shining in full stage light becomes all the more luminous.

Like Grace Kelly announcing her on-screen identity as Lisa … Carole … Freemont by turning on three lights one-by-one in Jimmy Stewart's apartment in *Rear Window* (Alfred Hitchcock, 1954), the personas of both Dietrich and Monroe as the showgirls Helen and Lorelei are communicated through the presence and absence of the light that shines upon them. In 1955 Joseph von Sternberg, director of *Blonde Venus*, recalled Dietrich's relationship with film lighting. His comments suggest that Dietrich was acutely aware of the power of light to shape and reinforce star status.

> While working with me, Miss Dietrich became so conscious of the value of light that her emotions dwindled when the lights snapped off one by one and the stage became dark, and when she walked past the power house, where the final switch was pulled to stop the dynamo, she felt as if she had received a blow.[5]

In these films lighting is the silent voice of a character's emotions, marking the highs and lows of experience, as well as an expression of star status, guiding and sculpting our view, constructing the codes of identification and love that lead to continued adoration. As Dietrich knew all too well, in order to maintain their existence on-screen, a star must continually shine.

Revelation

Anticipating the arrival of a star is one of the great joys of cinema spectatorship. That moment of recognition when a familiar, eagerly awaited face or body becomes visible for the first time elicits excitement. A star's entrance brings to mind all their previous incarnations on and off the screen, producing a heady mix of nostalgia and an expectation of the new in a dramatic moment of pure cinematic power. Delaying a star's entrance only increases the emotional force of the introduction. The longer the wait, the greater the anticipation; the bigger the star, the more intense the experience of recognition becomes. *The Third Man* (Carol Reed, 1949) and *Apocalypse Now* (Francis Ford Coppola, 1979) contain famously late big-star arrivals. Each film uses light as a vivid method of revelation and identification. The protagonists of both films – Holly Martins (Joseph Cotten) and Captain Benjamin L. Willard (Martin Sheen) – are searching, as is the spectator, for a man and for the truth. It is a search that is defined by the qualities and allusions of light; a search for knowledge and illumination, a search for a star.

The scene, almost two-thirds of the way through *The Third Man*, that precedes Harry Lime's (Orson Welles) first appearance, contains a number of overt hints – each one communicated with light – that suggest his entrance is imminent. Anna (Alida Valli), Harry's girlfriend, lies on her bed in the almost dark, mourning the apparent loss of her lover. Two spotlights beam down from above. The first illuminates her contemplative face in the darkness, highlighting her sadness; the second shines down on the large embroidered initials on her borrowed pyjamas that read 'H.L.'. The moment is at once an overt declaration of her continued love and a suggestion of Harry's

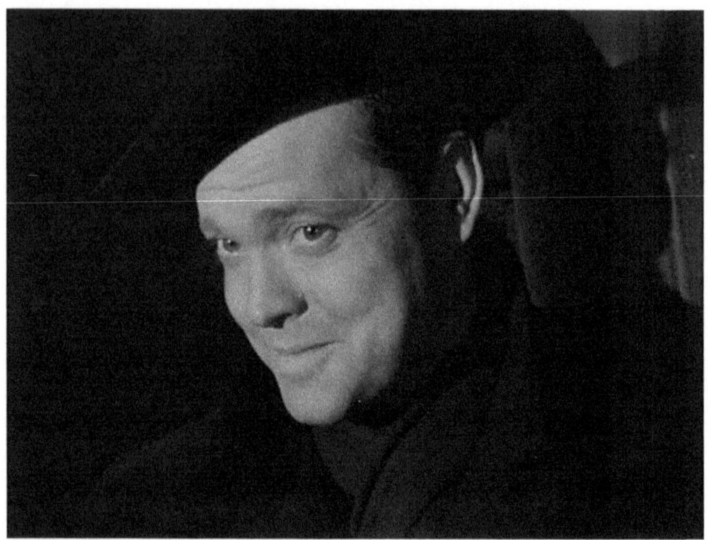

5   *The Third Man.* An unexpected light reveals Harry Lime's
(Orson Welles) identity

virtual proximity. He is no longer an absent suggestion; his
name, and with it his existence, has been lit up on the screen.
After Major Calloway (Trevor Howard) has convinced Holly
of Harry's involvement in a murderous black-market medicine
racket, Holly returns to Anna's apartment drunk and defeated.
He has brought her flowers tied up with a piece of string that
he uses to try to entice her cat into play. Holly wonders at
the cat's bored indifference: 'Not very sociable, is he.' Anna
explains the cat's reticence: 'No, he only liked Harry.' The cat
escapes through the window. While Anna and Holly continue
to discuss the revelations about Harry, the camera swoops
through the plants on the windowsill, pushing them apart like
a hand moving through the undergrowth, apparently searching
for the startled man on the dark street below. He runs into a
doorway, hiding from the camera's gaze. Outside, the cat pads
around a corner and sidles up to the hidden man's shoes that

poke out into the light, so that along with the strings of the famous theme by Anton Karas that increase in volume and pulsate in intense anticipation, his identity begins to become clear. Inside Holly moves to the window and places his hand on the light switch while he explains his decision to move on: 'I don't care whether Harry was murdered by Kurtz or Popescu or the third man. Whoever killed him there was some sort of justice.' At the exact moment he mentions the third man, he switches the light off and on again to emphasise his point; again light suggests a connection between Harry and the mysterious title character.

Holly sways drunkenly outside in the midnight streets after Anna rejects him. A cut reveals the continued presence of the man in the doorway: his shoes and the cat entwined around them are just visible in the street light. The cat meows. Holly becomes aware he is being watched. He shouts at the man, mistakenly believing he is a spying detective, goading him to 'step out in the light.' The noise wakes up a woman in a nearby apartment who turns on her bedroom light. Instantly, Harry's face, and with it Welles' star persona, is illuminated for the first time in the film. It is an immediate, precise moment of cinematic revelation. The camera zooms closer, Harry smiles, Holly calls out his friend's name in surprise. Cloaked in darkness, wearing a black hat, coat and scarf, the whiteness of Welles' familiar soft round face with its inquiring eyes and smirking mouth, combines with the unwavering intensity of the bedroom light and his delayed appearance, to produce a dramatic instant of emotive force. Like Jeanne's face in *La passion de Jeanne d'Arc*, when paired with the close-up, movie lighting of this kind isolates the face, drawing it closer to the screen, emphasising (his) presence. As quickly as it is revealed, Harry's face returns to darkness when the woman turns off her light and goes back to bed. Determined to keep his friend in sight, Holly dashes across the street, and is almost (somewhat ironically, considering it mirrors Harry's previously assumed fate) run over by a speeding car. Harry's feet in flight echo in the dark. A dramatic chiaroscuro chase sequence begins. It is not, however, Harry whom Holly runs after: it is Harry's shadow. As much as light previously revealed his identity, now it becomes his embodiment. Holly does not chase a man, but rather a man's trace; an ephemeral projection of a body cast with light. In this way *The Third Man* plays with the notion of the star as a transient mythical entity. Like Holly, we have waited a long time to see Harry/Welles, have eagerly anticipated this moment of revelation, only to be denied his prolonged presence and presented with a shadowy insubstantial approximation. As Holly explains to Calloway, 'I followed his shadow, until suddenly, well …. he vanished.' The remark is as much a comment on Holly's immediate situation, as it is a reference to the intangible nature of stardom itself.

Through fragmentary illumination, *Apocalypse Now* presents Colonel Walter E. Kurtz (Marlon Brando) as similarly unknowable. Unlike Holly in *The Third Man*, Captain Willard has known the identity of the man he is searching for since the film's start. By the time he reaches his target three-quarters of the way through the film, hidden deep in the jungle, at the height of the Vietnam War, the renegade Kurtz has reached epic mythical status as a brutally insane godlike dictator. Delay has increased his notoriety along with our eagerness to see him. After arriving at the mouth of the river and getting beaten in the mud, Willard is dragged into Kurtz's cave-like residence. Darkness reigns. Torchlight glints off lustrous arcane surfaces; blood, sweat and wet mud shine. Coppola conceals Kurtz in the gloom for as long as possible. The yellow light is redirected so that we, along with Willard, can initially only see the top of Kurtz's smoothly shaven sweating head. Illumination teases expectation. Brando's voice strikes the first chord of recognition. Willard's wide eyes glow white-hot, on fire in the darkness of the mud that surrounds them, straining, like the spectator, in impatient anticipation of Kurtz's imminent exposure. Still Coppola denies facial revelation. With every move, Kurtz's identity is concealed by shadow: he is dismembered by the

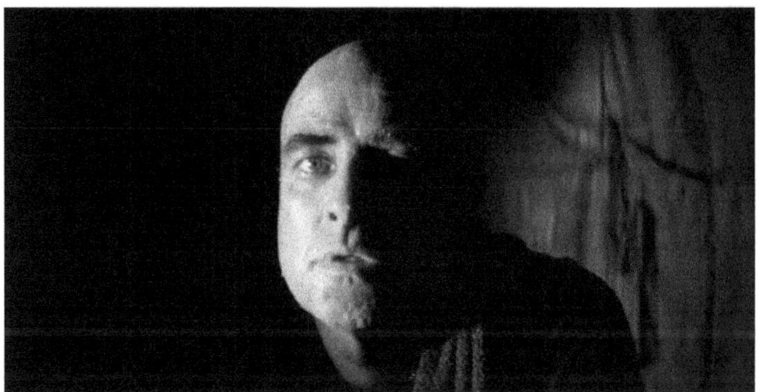

6 *Apocalypse Now.* Kurtz (Marlon Brando) pushes his face into the light

light, a vision in pieces. Kurtz sits on the bed, his body partially illuminated, his head hanging, face hidden, lost in thought. Flickering on the stone wall, Willard's continued presence is noted in shadow. Kurtz washes his face in a bowl of water; light drips through his fingers, hands linger, masking expression. Finally, tenderly, he presses his face forward allowing the light to wash across its surface before once more retreating. As quickly as he is sculpted, he vanishes. This is only a partial sighting.

Kurtz asks Willard if he is an assassin. Willard replies: 'I'm a soldier.' Angered, Kurtz now seems unable to remain hidden. He forces his head out of the shadows and for the first time we see fully lit features, sweat dripping, eye light glinting: a star reborn. 'You're neither.' He replies. 'You're an errand boy sent by grocery clerks to collect a bill.' The direction and strength of the light transforms Kurtz into a head without a body, a thought without a soul: a physical manifestation of pure ideology. As he moves in and out of the light, playing a game of cat and mouse with his own cinematic revelation, Kurtz/ Brando appears more myth than man. Kurtz's indecipherability – his confused mental state as a genius or a madman (or both)

– is communicated, as is Harry's moral ambiguity in *The Third Man*, via hesitant illumination. Each man attempts to avoid the light, shining brightly before melting into darkness; complete identification is ultimately unattainable.

Individuality

The light that falls upon the female protagonist at the centre of *Morvern Callar* (Lynne Ramsay, 2002) constantly changes, combining the sympathetic, stark eye lighting of *La passion de Jeanne d'Arc*, and the iconic, sensual lighting of *Blonde Venus* and *Gentlemen Prefer Blondes*, with the transient, nebulous illumination of Harry Lime and Colonel Kurtz. Using various lighting techniques *Morvern Callar* exemplifies a post-millennial shift in the luminous representation of both women and stars. Samantha Morton plays Morvern, a disillusioned young supermarket worker living in Scotland who finds her boyfriend dead on the kitchen floor of their flat. While trying to come to terms with his suicide, Morvern discovers a novel he has written and claims it as her own before dismembering and secretly burying his body and using the funeral money he has saved to fund a holiday to Spain. As we strive to understand Morvern's decisions, the texture and intensity of her light waxes and wanes alongside our indecisive sympathies. Uncertainty is intentional. Lighting in this film communicates a complex version of individuality and female identity at the turn of the millennium, drawing together shifting lighting styles and their suggestive meaning from across cinematic history.

Morvern is lost in the depths of her own psyche, frequently alone, curled up in the dark, her pale face at times lit up by pulses of recurring electric light that work as external representations of her fragmented mental state. At the start of the film Morvern's face looms out of the darkness, framed in extreme close-up, illuminated in pulses of warm yellow light that appear a slow heartbeat apart. The periods of blackness between the almost static images make the moments when her face appears seem like extended individual photographs. Like Kurtz in *Apocalypse Now* and Harry in *The Third Man*, lighting plays a game of hide-and-seek with her identity. Morvern caresses a man's body, stroking his arms and hands, kissing his neck and hair. Her fingers lightly touch his slashed wrist, the congealed blood working as the first indication that her lover is dead. As the screen goes black once again, Morvern's name, the title of the film, appears a word at time: large white letters brightly punctuate the surrounding blackness stamping her identity on the frame. A cut reveals a medium shot of their flat; the rhythmic, intermittent lights of a small Christmas tree illuminate pools of blood in the kitchen, shining down on the two figures on the floor; Morvern curled up like a foetus, her boyfriend face down in his own blood. Again, intermittent light denotes an uncertain introduction.

In the bath, Morvern thinks. Here the lighting is fluorescent; there is nowhere to hide. Her eyes are wide, red-rimmed with the pain of her loss. As the pool-playing man in the pub suggests later, when he shouts in her direction 'this time we're playing for Joan of Arc', in this scene Morvern looks just like Dreyer's depiction of Jeanne. Morton's soft, round face gazes up at us in mute despair. Sympathy is encouraged. Ramsay beautifies the image; light reflects off wet skin and bath water, shimmering in poetic pools of electric illumination. As she disappears under the water, again she curls up like a foetus and we are reminded of her tender age, a womanly body, retreating into childlike gesture under unwavering, accusatory strip lights.

Morvern and her best friend Lana (Kathleen McDermot) go to a house party in the Scottish countryside. Inside, the lighting makes it impossible for Morvern (and us) to forget what has happened: soft pink, red and yellow hues directly recall the Christmas tree lights currently illuminating her dead boyfriend on the floor in their flat. Escaping, she leaves the house and walks outside into the black night. The film slows down, stripped back to the grain, almost unable to take in or

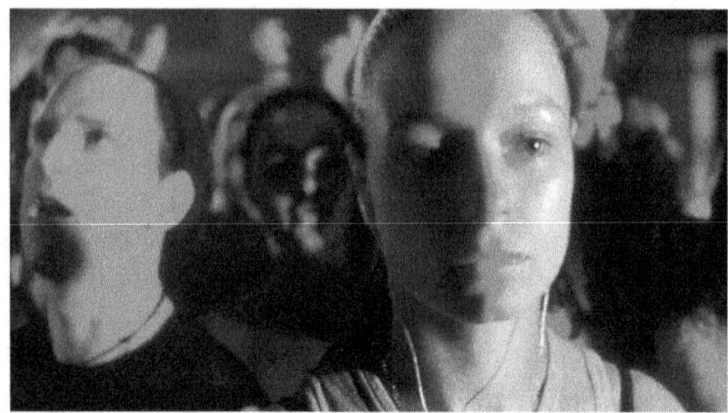

7 *Morvern Callar.* Pulsating red club lights isolate Morvern's (Samantha Morton) face

transmit sufficient light. On the waters of the loch, a man on a fishing boat shines a torch towards the bank. Morvern, dressed all in black, her pale face and skin blanched white against the darkness, stands watching him, before lifting up her skirt and displaying her knickers and suspenders. In this moment, Morvern shows that like Helen/Dietrich in *Blonde Venus*, she has a visceral relationship to light, basking in it, aggressively letting it fall on her body, mirroring the desiring gaze of the man on the boat with her brazen luminous power.

For Morvern, like Kurtz and Harry, darkness is safety. She hides herself away in it, seeks solace in its isolation, even though pinpoints of electric light continue to ensure that she remains unable to forget. One night in Spain, alone on the dance floor of a local club, Morvern is plunged into darkness. The red-blue lights return in pulsating waves that shudder and swell in time to the pumping music. Morvern is caught in blasts of bloody light that burst upon the screen like a camera's flash and envelop her in high-speed moments of static contemplation, illuminating her poetic intangibility. As a woman and a character she seems unreachable. At the end of the film, Morvern returns to the dark, red, womb-like isolation of the club. This time, however, in delayed photographic slow motion, as she moves and shifts in time to the pulsating lights, she seems for the first time content. As the lines of 'Dedicated to the One I Love' announce 'and the darkest hour is just before dawn', she looks directly at the camera, reborn, as though she has finally come to terms with both the inescapable nature of her loss and guilt, as well as her identity as a complex transitional character, unravelling the cinematic star codes of sympathy, desire and revelation, her face alternately cosseted in darkness and brought into being in the light.

Notes

1 R. Dyer, *White* (London and New York: Routledge, 1997), p. 102.
2 J. Alton, *Painting with Light* (London: University of California Press [1949], 1995), p. 29.
3 Dyer, *White*, p. 8.
4 *Ibid.*, p. 102.
5 J. von Sternberg, 'More Light', *Sight & Sound*, 25(2) (1955–56), 73.

2   Authenticity

No more confectionery: we're going to shoot in real
light.

(Jean-Luc Godard, cited by Raoul Coutard,
'Light of Day', *Sight & Sound*, 35(1) (1966))

The sun is beautiful.

(Michel (Jean-Paul Belmondo), *Breathless*)

'Real' light

The cinema does not precisely replicate reality. It is a medium
of observation, transformation and temporal manipulation.
Through a lens or on-screen, the world is not captured or
presented authentically, exactly as we see it, since the act of
recording and editing itself transforms the essence of that
which is filmed into something other than our experience of
'real' life. This is as much the case with the cinema's use and
depiction of light as it is regarding its manipulation of the other
tenets of *mise-en-scène*. As Christian Metz has noted, 'Realism
is not reality.'[1] This is not to say, however, that the *appearance*
of authentic illumination has not been consistently needed
and sought throughout cinematic history. From cinema's
earliest manifestations 'natural' light has been harnessed and
redirected, squeezed and channelled in order to illuminate

actors, props and sets, creating the expressive, atmospheric contrasts of drama as well as the flat illusion of softly diffused realism. In the late nineteenth century, outdoors under bright skies, the pioneers of early cinema struggled to harness enough light to make visible in the moving image that which they could see with their own eyes. A move indoors just a few years later offered freedom from the constraints of the limited and shifting hours of daylight. The glass roof of Edison's 1892 Black Maria studio could rotate to give the illusion of constant and consistent sunlight detached from its 'natural' shifting wax and wane, while in 1897 in Georges Méliès's spacious greenhouse-like studio, the searing light of the noon-day sun streaming through the vast panes of glass was diffused and redirected at will with thin strips of cotton material.[2] The very act of harnessing and focusing the light, however, changed its nature. In each of these production environments authenticity was required and often desired but the difficulties involved in attempting to capture a specific intensity of daylight as it incessantly grew brighter or dimmer with the arc of the sun, as well as the impact of unpredictable weather conditions, at times proved insurmountable and artificial light was eventually incorporated.[3] In an attempt to depict light both as it is and as it can be imagined, these early pioneers ended up controlling, directing and mastering illumination, creating a luminous spectacle out of the everyday, as opposed to an exact replication of light as it is experienced in nature.

With this in mind, this chapter is not an investigation of the use of natural light in the cinema, but rather a discussion of the way this light has been harnessed, framed, reconstructed and redirected in order to offer an impression of authenticity. As Mike O'Pray has suggested, 'cinematic realism is not a lack of artifice but rather the use of artifice to reveal the reality of the world seen through a camera's lens'.[4] In this context natural light can be understood as any kind of cinematic illumination that resembles light as it appears in nature. Gone are the bold abstractions of dramatic arc lights and the desiring sculptures of movie lighting. In their place we find a preference for outdoor spaces and the stark light of the noon-day sun. Characters wake in the hopeful light of dawn and party or sleep in darkness; the arc of their narratives is structured in days filled with sunrises and sunsets, experiencing accordant emotions that brighten and dim, that seek to mirror our own.

I have chosen to discuss key films from a range of waves and movements across cinematic history by filmmakers that have positioned themselves aesthetically and/or politically in opposition to apparently 'artificial' or 'old' cinematic traditions that either preceded them in a national context, or that were being contemporaneously celebrated in other parts of the world (in Hollywood for example). While these films are among the most discussed and studied in film history, it is hoped that a less traditional focus on their use of light will reveal new connections, while at the same time suggesting that the natural illumination they harness and project in some way reinforces and explains their position in the canon. In this vein, from Italian neo-realism I will look at *Bicycle Thieves* (Vittorio De Sica, 1948), from the French new wave (*nouvelle vague*), *Breathless* (Jean-Luc Godard, 1960), from the British new wave or 'kitchen sink' drama, *A Taste of Honey* (Tony Richardson, 1961) and from Dogme 95, *The Celebration* (Thomas Vinterberg, 1998). As Richard T. Kelly notes in his discussion of Dogme 95, at certain moments in cinematic history artificial tropes have been rejected in favour of new realistic ideals:

> All revolutions in art, the playwright David Hare argues, are a return to realism. Abstract painters and sculptors might beg to differ, but for cinema the claim clearly has integrity. At regular intervals in the medium's short history, particular film-makers have revolted against cinema's extravagant artifice, its wilful estrangement from life as it is lived. Instead they have proposed the camera as a tool to record and expose the world truly as it is.[5]

The films in this chapter use naturalistic lighting techniques and available light sources in various ways to present modern, stripped-back characters that are indelibly connected to their socio-historical positions, while projecting energetic, authentic, recognisable emotions. There is a (frequently political) desire in these films to break with established cinematic codes and conventions, to be vibrant, fresh and new, to be free from overtly stylised props and sets, to depict the world as it is and people as they are. Although the cinematography of each film is distinct (the improvisational aesthetic of *Breathless* with its long takes, jumpcuts and stylised acting, stands in stark opposition to the more formal, tempered register of the images and anti-acting of *Bicycle Thieves*, for example), they each flood their scenes with 'natural' light that illuminates apparently 'real' spaces in order to evoke genuine experiences that engage with notions of spontaneity and authenticity.

At the same time, light in each of these films continues to be guided, directed and sculpted in a distinctly artificial manner that seeks to reveal interior character psychology while emulating the beauty of the everyday, creating a cinematic spectacle from seemingly authentic light sources. The temporal motion of the sun as it rises and sets on-screen is of interest here, especially its reflection of a certain kind of natural harmony in which the vibrancy of day becomes the lethargy and fear of night, as well as the way strange optical tricks and quirks of 'natural' light are harnessed for their capacity to simultaneously connote genuine experience and evocative, expressive emotion. In these films characters are placed in specific situations on location in which light is channelled and redirected by buildings and architectural structures that epitomise their internal psychological states. Ultimately, an artificial version of 'real' life is constructed from the authentic illusion of 'real' light.

The passage of time

All the films in this chapter begin on location outdoors under bright daytime skies. Each opening scene encapsulates the drives and desires of their protagonists, positioning them as indelibly fixed to both their environment, and within it, their socio-economic position. At the same time, the particular qualities of the sun itself and the cycle of life it evokes as it travels across the sky either emphasises or counterbalances the emotional thrust of the scenes.

In *Bicycle Thieves*, under the stark white light of the Italian midday sun, unemployed men gather around a bus as it arrives in the dusty no-man's land between their sun-bleached apartment blocks. The men are desperate for jobs, eagerly following a government official as he disembarks with news of work. He only has a job for Ricci, however, a man who has grown so despondent that he ignored the bus and must be roused from despair by the desiccated roadside. Ricci's hopes are raised and then dashed within seconds. There is a job for him as a bill-poster, but to fulfil the requirements of the position, he must have a bicycle, a bicycle that he has recently pawned in order to buy food for his family. Through these sparse interactions and revelations, the predicaments that blight and enrich Ricci's life are concisely revealed: the omnipotent power of the state to manipulate the lives of its workers; the remorseless vagaries of chance and fate; the struggle to hope amidst despair; the force of familial love. In this luminous midday scene, where shadows shorten and dust fills the air, where the light strikes off the vast whitewashed tower blocks and scorches the earth, the dual qualities of the Italian sun as it warms and gives life while burning with unforgiving intensity, come to represent both De Sica's unflinching anti-fascist humanism, his struggle to reveal life as it is, and the unrelenting control of the state over the lives of its impoverished subjects.

An entire day elapses during the first six minutes of *Breathless*. At 10.50 a.m., Michel Poiccard (Jean-Paul Belmondo) steals a car in the centre of Paris and leaves the city at speed. Dressed in a Trilby and tie, in homage to the American gangster movies Godard so admired, Michel smokes and fiddles with the radio while espousing his hatred of other drivers and love for the countryside. The joy and freedom of the open road is echoed in the buzz of his engine and the riffs and flows of the upbeat jazz score as he overtakes cars and rushes beneath sunlit trees, slicing their definite shadows with his wheels, racing through time in accelerated, experimental jumpcuts. After ignoring two female hitchhikers who are apparently too ugly to pick up, he starts to play with a gun he has found in the dashboard. 'Pap; pap, pap, pap', he shouts as he waves the gun in the air, pointing it at himself in the mirror and out of the window, spotting his first luminous target. 'C'est beau du soleil' ('The sun is beautiful') he exclaims before shooting it. The sound of the gun goes off; sunlight scatters through the trees. Atmospherically, his act splits the sequence in two. Before, he flew down the road undeterred, enjoying his liberty in the bright sunshine; after, he is annoyed to be held up by roadworks amidst extending shadows and dimming daylight. As the light leaves, his mood darkens and his luck fails. The police catch him overtaking a truck near the roadworks and chase him on motorbike. Michel stops down a lane in the fading light and struggles to restart his car before he is caught. One of the policemen pulls off the road to arrest him. Panicking, Michel shoots him with the gun from the dashboard and runs off through twilit fields past the setting sun as it seems to die in the sky from his bullet, echoing the fate of the policeman on the ground.

Similarly, the joys and sorrows of the protagonists in *A Taste of Honey* and *The Celebration* are encapsulated during the brief moments they spend outdoors in daylight at the start of each film. In *A Taste of Honey*, Jo's (Rita Tushingham) adolescent personality is laid bare in a bright schoolyard as she plays netball with a group of fellow schoolgirls and an overenthu-siastic gym teacher. As the other girls run and jump, catching and passing with ease, Jo's arms flail and she continually drops the ball, until she becomes so frustrated, she lashes out and punches it into the air on purpose, much to the annoyance of her teacher. Throughout the light is clear and strong, creating shadows from the players that cast definite shadows on the tarmac, echoing Jo's stubborn determination and strength of character: an iron will that constantly gets her into and out of trouble during the course of the film.

In a long shot, Christian (Ulrich Thomsen) walks down a hazy undulating road towards his father's house in *The Celebration*. The distance between him and the camera transforms him into a tiny grey figure in a vast rural landscape. On either side of the road golden hay sways in the breeze, filling the screen with the soft feverish haze of a molten-brown summer's day. In his white shirt and grey check city suit he seems displaced, mentioning his awe at the beauty of his father's land to the person on the other end of his mobile phone. The film cuts abruptly to a close-up shot of the back of Christian's head as he continues to talk. It must be around midday since the sunlight overhead is so intense that he squints as he looks out across the fertile fields. The first of the Dogme 95 films, when it was released in 1998 the quality of *The Celebration*'s digital cinematography, transferred to 35 mm film, shot without artificial lighting techniques, was ground-breaking.[6] At times in this opening scene the image appears blown out and overexposed; an unavoidable (and desired) realistic result of shot-on-the-fly hand-held digital filmmaking that only serves to intensify the almost sickly saturated sunshine of this apparently utopian summer's day. The arrival of Christian's brother Michael (Thomas Bo Larsen) with his wife and a car full of children shatters any sense that this is a rural idyll. When he sees Christian walking along the roadside with his suitcase, Michael reverses the car at speed and orders his wife and children to get out so that he can give his brother a lift. Michael is brash, arrogant and offensive; a stark counterpoint to mild-mannered Christian, who visibly flinches when Michael pinches his cheek in a false gesture of brotherly affection. The scene becomes increasingly uncomfortable when Michael, still in jovial older-brother mode, jumps on Christian's back in a mock wrestle and exclaims 'I could fuck you right here.' The unnerving incestuous joke proves portentous within the narrative of child abuse and recrimination that follows, while the effusive sunlight shining off the pastoral beauty that surrounds them works as a counterpoint to the growing sense of familial unrest.

These bright, naturalistic opening scenes in which we meet the films' protagonists for the first time condense characterisation and narrative meaning into a few brief moments. Visual shorthand suggests the characters' pasts and problems, fears and desires. Perhaps with the exception of *Breathless* (whose protagonist is figured somewhat fantastically, and within which the sun itself seems to die) the recognisable outdoor settings in which the protagonists stories begin to unfold in familiar, uncontrollable, unpredictable daylight emphasises the realism of their portrayals and situations.

The passage of the sun from morning until night is reflected throughout these films in which the vital positivity of dawn transitions into the dark despair of night. Here the metaphor of the sun's arc is stretched to its full extent. In *Bicycle Thieves* after Ricci's wife sells their bedlinen in order to buy back his bicycle, the early morning twilight brings hope for the family. As dawn breaks, father and son cycle to work in identical outfits, happy and smiling, they join the procession of other men with bicycles and jobs. Lit by the rising sun, excitement and joy extend alongside their stretched shadows on the road. By the end of the day, however, the bike has been stolen and father and son descend into despondency. The diminishing light reflects their loss of faith.

The large family party that Christian is walking towards in bright sunlight at the start of *The Celebration*, transitions from tense daytime familial affection into the horrifying disclosure of terrible deeds at night. After Christian reveals during his dinner speech that his father sexually abused him and his twin sister when they were children, the strange, frightening atmosphere that is often associated with the hours of darkness is employed to startling effect. During his outburst, the sun is setting. Light diffuses through the soft gauze of the window drapes, but candles are lit, night is on its way. Christian is removed from the dining room and ejected from the house a number of times, but on each occasion he returns to reiterate his accusations more forcefully. Finally, his sister Helene confirms the abuse to the stunned guests via a letter written by Christian's twin before she died. Night closes in as Helene reads. The encroaching darkness outside shrinks their world to the enclosed space of the candlelit room, reflecting the darkening mood of the stunned guests sitting stricken in their seats. The support of his present and departed sisters acts as a catalyst for both Christian's absolution and Helge's rejection. After the guests retire to bed, in the dark Christian encounters a positive vision of his dead sister, while Michael beats his abusive father Helge on the lawn. The next day an icy-blue Danish morning dawns as birds fly over the family estate. Inside the guests are eating breakfast. Christian is reintegrated with the rest of his family, joking again with Michael and smiling when his waitress girlfriend Pia agrees to move with him to Paris. The positivity of the bright morning light is momentarily diffused when Helge and his wife Else arrive. Michael refuses to let his daughter sit on his father's knee, Helge apologises, but it is no use, he realises that none of his family will ever speak to him again. Michael banishes Helge from the breakfast table; he is disgraced and finally atones for what he has done.

Throughout all these films the motion of the sun through the sky and the resultant quality of light has either reinforced or offset the actions and emotions of the scenes. As the cinematographer John Alton asserted, on-screen in each of these cinematic moments, 'A sunrise creates a certain encouraging feeling. A sunset symbolises the close of a cycle.'[7]

Natural phenomena

As much as these films rely upon the arc of the sun to authenticate their narratives, they also make use of unusual quirks of natural light as a way to beautify the image. These dramatic natural phenomena, including variable weather conditions, sunspots and twilight, at once validate the scenes with realism (reflecting as they do the reaction of our own eyes to shifting lighting conditions) and add evocative, poetic resonance to images that otherwise lack the audacious artifice of constructed illuminated spectacle. Alongside the realistic tropes of intense, atmospheric natural light, and often in the absence of professional studio lights, these films rely upon the fantastic effects of hand-held lights by characters on location, such as torches, candles, lighters and sparklers that are used in dark naturalistic settings to widen the extent of available light sources and as an alternative means of expressive illumination. Throughout, a sense of wonder at the light of the natural world, along with humanity's ability to harness and replicate such luminous energy, is emphasised.

Still engaged in the futile search for their stolen bicycle in *Bicycle Thieves*, Ricci and his son Bruno get a lift in a truck to the local market, hoping that they will catch the thief trying to make a quick sale. The once-stark Italian sunlight ominously dims as the truck rolls along the cobbled streets. Nearing their destination, raindrops spatter on the window of the cab, increasing in intensity as Ricci and Bruno get out and are caught in a downpour. All around them men run and cycle to get out of the rain. Clutching at the feeble protection offered by their jackets, father and son desperately cast about for the bike and for help. Neither is forthcoming. The rain sluices down on them in strident silver bars, battering their bodies until they are drenched through. Water pools on the streets and in Ricci's hat. In the subdued light, when all around is cloaked in grey, Ricci's soaked jacket becomes a singular beacon of reflection, desperately bouncing back any light that clings to it, in an echo

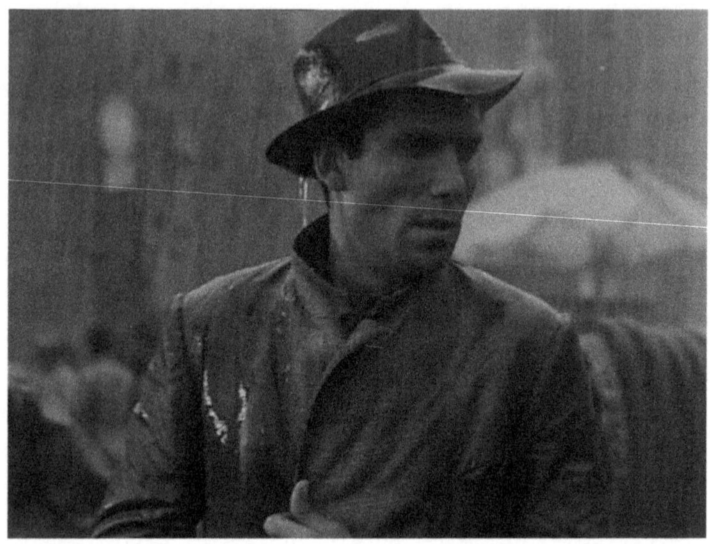

8   *Bicycle Thieves/Ladri di biciclette*. Ricci's (Lamberto Maggiorami) jacket resolutely reflects the light during a downpour

of his own resolute determination. As the rain stops and the sun returns, Ricci spots the thief and the bike; hope glimmers in the light, but is almost immediately extinguished when the young man rides off without being caught.

The fourth rule of Dogme 95's 'ten vows of chastity' states: 'The film must be in colour. Special lighting is not acceptable. (If there is too little light for exposure the scene must be cut or a single lamp may be attached to the camera.)' A number of techniques are employed in *The Celebration* in order to stay within the strict Dogme 95 manifesto, while evocative cinematic light continues to be used for expressive effect. Although additional light sources are, for the most part, avoided, on multiple occasions, the lighting *can* be considered to some extent 'special'. The brief title sequence opens with a striking extreme close-up of light sparkling on water. Glittering diamonds of yellow light swim across the screen. A cut retreats to reveal the Danish title of the film, *Festen*, hovering indeterminately, a scratched black scrawl beneath the translucent surface of the water. The opalescent, handmade simplicity of writing on paper beneath liquid anticipates the stripped-back creative spontaneity of the digital filmmaking that follows. As Christian finishes his conversation at the start of the film and puts his mobile phone back in his pocket, the camera films him in a head-on close-up walking resolutely down the hot road. The sun sits high in the sky, its angle creating multiple coloured sunspots on the camera's lens that cascade across his face and the screen. The effect beautifies the image with the striking transformative qualities of natural light and colour, recalling the lustrous abstract light of the film's titles while simultaneously verifying the apparent reality of the filmic world. Beauty and realism combine.

The quality of the light in *The Celebration* constantly shifts and shimmers, not just with the passage of time, but because of the oscillating nature of high-grain digital cinematography. At times characters' faces are barely distinguishable in the back of cabs or in the gloom of the house because sources of light on location are unavailable, inaccessible or inappropriate. In these moments when light leaves the frame, tension heightens and darkness becomes connotative of character interiority. As the family disintegrates, the screen degrades into irregular jagged pixels that lack the visual glue of illumination. When Christian faints in front of the concierge after his sister has read the letter, he almost disappears into the darkness of the screen; our struggle to see him reflects his struggle to deal with the events of the evening. Whilst unconscious he experiences visions of his dead sister holding a candle. With only a lighter for illumination he searches for her as she calls out to him from the gloom. In dramatic isolated flashes of flickering light his sister's smiling face is drawn out of the shadows. Illuminated by the expressive flame of his lighter they meet in a doorway and embrace, their blurred, barely visible expressions of joy melting into each other.

A similar technique is used in *A Taste of Honey* when Jo and her gay friend Geoffrey go on a trip to the countryside. Since the young black sailor who made Jo pregnant went back to sea, Jo and Geoff have set up house together in a small crumbling bedsit. In need of a break from the city just after Jo has found out she's pregnant, the pair race into the countryside. On the top of a hill with fields stretching around them, Geoff proposes and tries to kiss her. Reasserting her independence, Jo rejects him, before announcing she is going down to the caves: 'You're nothing to me', she says, 'I'm everything to meself.' Underground in the pitch-black, lamps and candles light their way. Stalactites loom out of the darkness, illuminated by sparse torchlight. Holding their candles directly in front of their faces, Jo and Geoff look at each other in a brief moment of shared intimacy, brought together by the darkness that surrounds them and the partial, tender candlelight. Away from the bright, natural light of the hilltop and the city, Jo finally feels able to answer Geoff's personal questions about the man that made her pregnant, admitting that she loved him, before exclaiming her hatred of love itself. The drama of the moment is exemplified by the dramatic contrasts of light and dark that surround them. Authentic light in a realistic setting proves intensely atmospheric, creating a philosophical, contemplative feeling that is echoed in the last shot of the film when Jo, now heavily pregnant, holds a sparkler in front of her face in the darkness and seems to contemplate the childhood she has lost and the child inside her about to be born.

In *The Celebration*, at dusk and dawn in the waning light the sense of psychic disruption and unintelligible action only intensifies. In order to shut Christian up after his speech, Michael and some other family members drag him outside and tie him to a tree in the woods on his father's land that he so admired at the start of the day. In dark-blue digital twilight, unaided by electric lighting equipment, Christian languishes in the gloom; his relationship with his relatives has apparently been completely destroyed; yet the momentary absence of his brutal family offers respite: the eerie quiet seems to afford him time to think. Similarly, on the other side of the eventful night, Michael beats his father at dawn. In shifting twilight Christian answers his mother's cries for help, placing a hand on his broken father, in a tender gesture of love that his father is incapable of reciprocating. The pale breaking light reflects both Christian's interstitial relationship with his father: his love and hatred for the shattered protector who abused him, and the fact that the family is in flux, tentatively emerging out of the darkness that almost destroyed them. In these films, the startling light of constructed artificial illumination is rejected in favour of the strange light of natural phenomena and the familiar flicker of recognisable light-giving objects. In each case the very act of filming and recording itself, along with the experimental techniques used, and the extreme emotions of the characters make everyday light seem remarkable, pushing the naturalistic image towards spectacle.

Light space

With the exception of the rural landscape of *The Celebration*, the architecture of the cities in which these films are shot offers a final means through which natural light is sculpted to emotive and spectacular effect. Buildings and architectural structures block, direct and re-frame daylight, creating patterns and pools of luminosity for the characters to interact with, shaping and marking their moods, whilst at night the electric, human-made lights of the city entice the eye, offering information and atmosphere as well as basic illumination.

One evening in *Breathless*, towards the start of the film, Michel buys a paper from a street vendor before turning around to see Patricia, the woman he loves, sitting in a car kissing another man. Michel has already called Patricia 'dégueulasse' (disgusting) because she wouldn't break her date to go out with him instead, so in frustration he has followed her. The kiss marks the moment Michel realises he must work harder to keep Patricia, as well as suggesting that he might not be able to fully trust her. As Patricia drives off with the other man, Michel watches them go, smoking and reading the paper while leaning on a car. Loitering in the twilight, around him the street lights of Paris atmospherically turn on section by section. Quite literally Michel seems to be having a 'light-bulb' moment, with the subtle ignition of faint radiance from the ornate metallic Parisian streetlights operating as an immediate visual indication of his growing suspicions. This instant of luminous revelation proves portentous, of course, when Patricia gives Michel up to the police at the end of the film, a move that ultimately costs him his life. Sometime later, electric lights in an authentic city setting again offer information. After Patricia and Michel hide out from the police in a cinema, she runs into a shop to buy a newspaper. The camera follows her as she enters the shop, pausing by the entrance as she goes inside, re-framing to centre on the flowing electronic display above the door that reads: 'Police closing in on Michel Poiccard'. The moving incandescent sign offers two kinds of information. Literally, it suggests Michel is about to be caught, heightening tension, upping the ante on an already tense chase sequence. Figuratively, it encapsulates the exciting modernity of the city, and by association, the film, displaying a new technological environment in which shifting electronic lights have become a fundamental part of the architecture of night-time city streets.

Architecture performs a similarly symbolic light-sculpting function in *A Taste of Honey*. Just before Jo and Geoff go off to the countryside, he finds her standing alone underneath the viaduct on the edge of town. In a long shot, the vast arch re-frames the view, carving a curved window from the earth and sky with bright daylight and dark bricks that shrink the friends into tiny silhouettes as they talk in echoed whispers. Below, the abject grey streets belching smoke and fumes, seem hazy and far away from this aptly magical and dramatic backdrop to Jo's revelations about her unplanned pregnancy. Panicking about

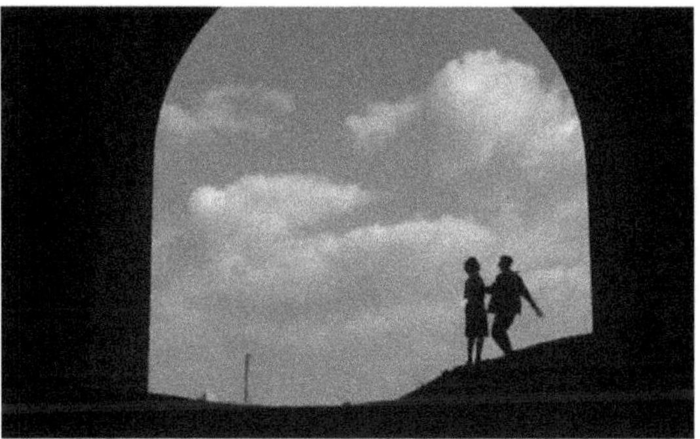

9   *A Taste of Honey.* Jo (Rita Tushingham) and Geoffrey
(Murray Melvin) are transformed into iconic silhouettes of
youthful exuberance

the prospect of motherhood, Jo runs up the slope to the back of
the arch, turning to face the camera, before flinging her arms in
the air and exclaiming, 'My usual self is a very unusual self, and
don't you forget that Geoffrey Ingham. I'm an extraordinary
person. There's only one of me, like there's only one of you!'
Behind Jo's head clouds blow across the archway, catching the
light and reflecting her shifting mood, like an extraordinary
light-filled moving painting. Geoff runs up the slope to join
her sudden jubilation, before they both alternately shout to the
world, 'We're unique!' 'Young!' 'Unrivalled!' 'Smashing!' 'We're
bloody marvellous!' As their silhouettes jump and embrace
in front of the bright curve of sky, the intense joy of their
exclamations combines with the visual drama of the setting
and the atmospheric natural light to produce a moment of pure
emotional force that once again pushes an otherwise naturalistic
film towards luminous spectacle.

One of the most evocative uses of architecture to redirect
light in *Bicycle Thieves* comes just after Ricci confronts the boy
who stole his bicycle, when the vivid quality of Italian sunlight
as it slants off the buildings overhead is used for symbolic
effect. Even though the thief has been caught, Ricci realises

that he does not have enough evidence to press charges, and so, in front of a policeman and a group of locals who are protecting the boy, he backs away from the situation, admitting defeat through gesture. As the local men shout and jeer in triumph, Ricci pushes them from his path in staccato shoves that resonate with the frustrated anger he is unable to direct towards the ineffective policeman and young thief. He strides towards the corner of the street, pausing momentarily to look back at the situation that has ruined his life, affording the camera a moment to push closer, amplifying his despair. On the other side of the wall he is filmed in a long shot from the end of the road as he beckons to Bruno to follow him. Hugging tight to the buildings on the right-hand side of the frame, the two of them walk in single file, their heads alternately glancing behind and hanging low in shifting states of fear and abject sorrow. The absolute desolation of the moment is driven home: all is lost. Beneath their feet, however, the buildings have divided the street with sunlight and shadow, so that while the rest of the cobbles languish in darkness, Ricci and Bruno's path is marked by a thin strip of dazzling natural illumination. This slice of sunshine that has forced its way to the ground through the tightly packed tenements above shimmers with optimism, since it seems to mark the path of a righteous man, a man who continues to rally for truth and justice in the face of dark adversity. It is a brief moment of luminous architecturally formed hope that makes the following scene of Ricci's bike-stealing fall from grace all the more devastating.

Although most of *Bicycle Thieves* is shot in daylight outdoors on the wide cobbled streets of Rome, light is consistently reshaped by human-made structures and by the men that surround them. In the opening scene, the vast stone housing blocks that surround Ricci's quest for work are turned white by the glaring sun, at once reflecting and sculpting the light into horizontal shadows that score the earth like smudged traces of the buildings laid flat. As the men gather, the space seems to open up from around and above, the height of the blocks leads the eye up and into the sky beyond, creating a sense of expansion that, as Mike O'Pray has noted, is not without irony, considering the predicament of Ricci's socio-economic entrapment:

> Something that passes without remark in Italian neo-realist films is the nature of their light, which is one of their most moving characteristics ... The opening shots of de Sica's famous *The Bicycle Thieves* is exemplary of this from the beginning of the film with its shots of the sunlight reflecting its perfect whiteness on the huge, white, flat-faced workers' buildings where Ricci awaits the employment lists. The intense sense of space which is open to the light, to human action, is marked in the film. Part of the bitter irony of *The Bicycle Thieves* is the impossibility of action within such spaciousness.[8]

There is, of course, a marked difference between internal and external shots in the film, since while space in the latter is extensive, in the former the lives of the Riccis in their box-like apartment, bartering through tiny windows at the pawnbrokers, or seeking help in the packed clairvoyant's bedroom and church, seem stifled and restricted, a condition that is intensified by the way these internal spaces are artificially, dimly lit and tightly framed, in contrast to the vast freedoms implied by the natural brightness of external sunlight. In fact, as the film progresses, as Ricci and Bruno's search for the bicycle gets increasingly desperate, even the outdoor spaces seem to close in on them, especially in the bustling market scenes, as streets get smaller and more crowded, or when Ricci finally finds the boy who stole the bicycle, only to be confronted by an angry mob who fill the screen with their bodies and animosity, soaking up the light. This sense of shrinking light and space becomes almost unbearable in the closing moments of the film when Ricci himself steals a bicycle, only to find that the once open road ahead has been closed off by angry, rushing men who surround, beat and humiliate him in front of his son. As Ricci and Bruno walk away from the camera in the dying moments of the film and disappear into the distance, their sad story is figured as one amidst hundreds, since they are surrounded by a tide of other men, dressed just like them, consuming the screen, each one heading in the same direction: towards the shrinking, fading, uncertain Italian light ahead.

In the absence of artificial lighting techniques, these films rely upon architectural structures and location illumination to reflect and manipulate available light sources as a means to project character interiority onto the screen. Realism does not necessitate the rejection of visual pleasure in *Bicycle Thieves*, or indeed in any of these films; rather the light of the natural world and the authentic drama of real settings are chosen precisely *because* of their ability to conjure striking moments of visual display that reflect and intensify emotion. As Andrew Higson has eloquently argued, although the British new wave films like *A Taste of Honey* eschew artificiality, the evocative beauty of their harsh cityscapes and natural light sources at times transcends actuality, merging the authenticity of real places with the artifice of cinematic space in moments of poetic realism that involve a 'more perfect conjunction of surface realism and moral realism, a conjunction which in fact *transcends* ordinariness, which makes the ordinary strange, beautiful – *poetic*'.[9]

In each of these films the light that illuminates the characters and sets, whether sunlight or streetlight, is both natural and spectacular. The light that hits Ricci as he waits to hear if he has work strikes the screen with the intense heat of the Italian noon-day sun. As Michel and Patricia wander down the Champs-Élysées, diffused rays flatly swirl around them in glamorous monochrome daylight. As Jo and Geoff dance and jump beneath oppressive, darkened arches, the bright sky beyond reflects their startling, hopeful exuberance. As Christian walks down the road to his father's house in *The Celebration*, sunlight fractures startling rainbow sunspots across the screen. Each lighting scenario is embraced for the authentic quality of its lighting conditions, not just the look of 'reality', but the recollection and replication of moments of spectacular natural light in the 'real' world that mirror or emphasise emotion, that stand out as special, powerful and worthy of our attention, that create a beautiful and poetic cinematic spectacle out of the everyday light that surrounds us.

Notes

1 C. Metz, *Film Language: A Semiotics of the Cinema* (New York: Oxford University Press, 1974), p. 21.
2 See B. Salt, *Film Style and Technology: History and Analysis 2nd Edition* (London: Starword, 1992), pp. 31–2.
3 See Georges Méliès's discussion on the difficulties of shooting with daylight in 'Cinematographic Views' (1906), in R. Abel (ed), *French Film Theory and Criticism: A History/Anthology 1907–1939, Vol. I* (Princeton, NJ: Princeton University Press, 1988), pp. 35–47, p. 40.
4 O'Pray, *Film, Form and Phantasy,* p. 193.
5 R. T. Kelly, in Pam Cook (ed), *The Cinema Book 3rd Edition* (London: BFI, 2007), p. 196.
6 See H. Willis, *New Digital Cinema: Reinventing the Moving Image* (London: Wallflower, 2005), pp. 24–9; R. Kelly, *The Name of this Book Is Dogme 95* (London: Faber and Faber, 2000).
7 Alton, *Painting with Light*, p. 120.
8 O'Pray, *Film, Form and Phantasy*, p. 212.
9 A. Higson, 'Space, Place, Spectacle: Landscape and Townscape in the "Kitchen Sink" Film', in Andrew Higson (ed), *Dissolving Views: Key Writings on British Cinema* (London: Cassell, 1996), pp. 133–56, p. 137.

3   The imaginary

I saw a street, lit as if in full daylight by neon lights and topping them, oversized, luminous advertising moving, turning, flashing on and off, spiralling … something which was completely new and near fairytale like for a European in those days, and this impression gave me the first thought of an idea for a town of the future.

> (Fritz Lang, overlooking Manhattan from the deck of the *SS Deutschland*, 1924)[1]

Oh my God – it's full of stars!

> (Lieutenant Bowman (Keir Dullea), *2001: A Space Odyssey*, 1968)

In the cinema it was 1902, not 1969, when man first went to the moon. Seeking to discover the secrets of the night sky, five astronomers climbed inside a bullet-shaped spaceship and embarked on a trip to the stars. As they rocketed into the fantastical heavens above, the vast white globe of the moon grew larger and brighter, until they were able to see the shining face of the man in the moon before crash-landing into his luminous pock-marked facade. This scene, from the middle of Méliès's famous *Le voyage dans la lune* (*A Trip to the Moon*, 1902), encapsulates the awe and wonder invoked by the style

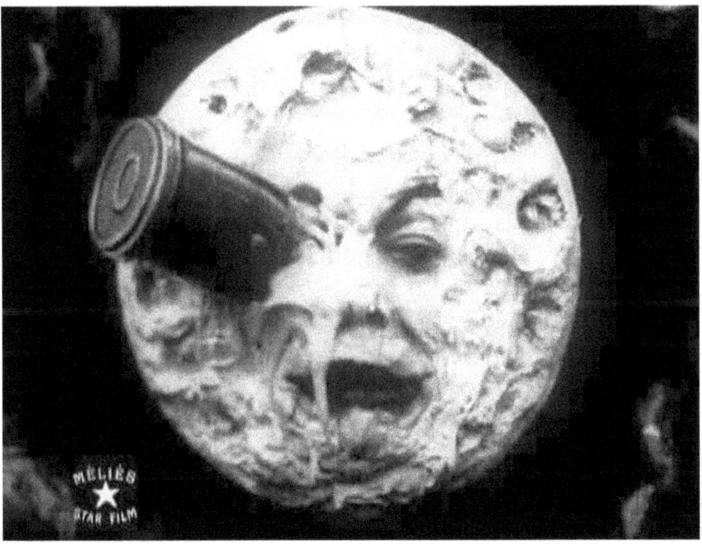

10 *A Trip to the Moon/Le voyage dans la lune*. Méliès's rocket blasts into the pock-marked facade of the moon

of cinematic lighting focused on in this chapter. In one of the first science-fiction films ever made, Méliès used sculptural sets, 'trick' shots and dramatic lighting techniques to transport viewers to another world. Light, sculpted and redirected, along with bursts of fire and puffs of smoke, became a key constituent of magic and illusion in the cinema. Dramatic illumination created spectacular effects.

Thematically, although comedic in tone, *Le voyage dans la lune* established many future preoccupations of science-fiction cinema. The wonder of the glowing moon in the dark sky above, the excitement and fear of the unknown, the ability to visualise a place that exists either beyond our physical reach or only in the realm of the imagination: all are tropes that have persisted in the cinema for over a hundred years from Méliès's films to the present day. As Tom Gunning has noted in an essay on *Le voyage dans la lune*, 'From almost its beginnings, cinema invoked the moon, as if the silvery light of the projector piercing through a dark theatre recalled lunar illumination.'[2] At the heart of this kind of cinema is the spectacle of light as a means to realise the fantastic, as a way to visualise and authenticate the landscapes and emotions of our imagination. Of course, as has been discussed in previous chapters, whether natural or artificial in origin, revealing a face at night or a city at dawn, light in the cinema is often used for spectacular effect. In the films discussed below, however, illumination, in the form of 'special effects', becomes both the substance and the solidified focus of the camera's gaze. It offers 'the possibility of "representing the unrepresentable"', of making the invisible visible, the immaterial material.[3] It gives the unknown form and context, existence and atmosphere.

In films like *Metropolis* (Fritz Lang, 1927), *Close Encounters of the Third Kind* (Steven Spielberg, 1977) and *The Matrix* (Andy and Larry Wachowski, 1999) light combines with science and technology to figure other beings and other worlds, from futuristic robotic artificial intelligence and flashing alien ships, to ubiquitous computer programs. In these films cities of the future scatter a thousand lit windows into the night sky, alien ships are constructed with pulsing coloured strobes and computers mark their infiltration into every corner of our lives in recognisable alternative worlds that seep a sick green haze across the screen. Similarly, when the camera turns away from what is 'out there' to what is 'in here', in films such as *An American in Paris* (Vincent Minnelli, 1951), *Vertigo* (Alfred Hitchcock, 1958) and *Three Colours: Blue* (Krzysztof Kieslowski, 1993), light visualises internal fantasy spaces and altered mental states, from effervescent joy and desolate sadness to jarring bouts of uncontrollable delirium. In these daydreams and memories and drug-induced confusions, emotions become so intense that they pour out of bodies, lighting up the frame with riotous shades of radiant feeling.

Whether expressing an uncanny exterior force or an interior psychic disruption, in this context transformative artificial light is embraced for its strange, vivid and, most of all, spectacular potential. These films present dramatic cinematic light as pure optical display, revelling in the visual pleasure of light itself. Inspired by the wondrous archaic luminosity of the stars in the night sky, against the black, bottomless backdrop of outer or inner space, cinematic light shines, pulsates and projects more brightly than it did before, pushing intense, arresting illumination through the screen, creating other worlds and externalising emotion, transporting us all elsewhere.

The future

Constructed with startling electric luminosity, the city of the future is a frequently imagined alternative cinematic world. Using the bustling metropolises of the twentieth century as their inspiration, filmmakers from Fritz Lang to Ridley Scott built towering infernos of the future with pyrotechnic special effects and stroboscopic bursts of dazzling light. Shot for dramatic effect against the inky night sky or in the gloomy depths of the earth, the bright artificiality of these imagined cityscapes appears all the more intense. Combining the visceral modernity of new technology with the archaic nostalgia of mythic narrative, these exciting, dangerous cities seem to embody our hopes and fears about our world as it might evolve beyond tomorrow. In scenes that pour light from the screen, these films make real an environment beyond our reach, transforming the cinematic realm into a virtual time machine with the ability to imagine the next stage of brightly lit human evolution.

Metropolis begins with shooting white searchlights that enter the screen from all sides, building the constructivist-style title from angular beams of geometric illumination, announcing its modernist intent from the start. Behind the title the city of the future is built from layered shapes and painted shadows juxtaposed at contrasting angles that add to the sense of collaged artificiality. Strobe light blasts upwards from the apex of skyscrapers, forming buildings and windows from light and shadow. As the fanfare shifts from riotous trumpeting to the racing rallies of drums and strings, the external structures fade into the whirring action of internal cogs and wheels that pump and shunt the city's power, shining brightly, intersecting and overlaid, giving the impression of motion, speed and functionality. As the screenwriter of *Metropolis* Thea von Harbou writes:

> Metropolis is a restlessly roaring ocean … with a surf of light … Slashed into cones and cubes by the mowing scythes of searchlights, the houses glowed, soaring, towering, and light flowed down their flanks like rain. The streets lapped up the glowing brightness. They, too, glowed, and all that glided along them in an incessant stream threw cones of light before it.[4]

Windows and walls, pavements and buttresses, pistons and cranks, title and city; everything in the opening moments of *Metropolis* seems to have been constructed with light. Here light is not just the means through which we view the image, nor it is merely the vehicle through which tone and mood is set, rather it is the substance out of which things on-screen are formed – light itself is the object of our vision. Of course, illumination as a mode of construction is not just used within cinematic cities; it is also a fundamental fixture of our own. Highways and advertising, cathedrals and office blocks, restaurants and cinemas; at night in the modern world each is created and designated with light. As Wolfgang Jacobsen and Werner Sudendorf argue, 'The cities of the 20th Century are born of light. Their architecture is structured, supported, and banked by lights … Neon, discovered at the beginning of the century, becomes a construction material like stone or concrete.'[5] Cinematic cities of the future use the ontological filmic propensity for luminosity and combine it with the way we light our cities at night, exaggerating electric technology to provide entire futuristic environments that glow, spark and flash from their lowest foundations to their highest spires.

Douglas Trumbull is a special-effects supervisor who has honed the craft of constructing alternative futuristic worlds and imaginary experiences with light. Responsible for the star-gate sequence in Stanley Kubrick's *2001: A Space Odyssey* (1968), the alien spacecrafts in Steven Spielberg's *Close Encounters of the Third Kind*, and (with 'visual futurist' Syd Mead) the innovative vision of a future Los Angeles in Ridley Scott's *Blade Runner* (1982), Trumbull is a cinematic lighting virtuoso.[6] Trumbull's skill lies in the way he uses cinematic light as a plastic medium akin to music, paint or clay. He sculpts mindscapes, aliens and cities with coloured illumination, blasting the viewer through time and space with painted swathes of vibrant luminosity and bursting stroboscopic communications that seem to give the 'other' or the 'otherworldly' tangible form and material composition. In Trumbull's visions of an alternative present or a conceivable future, light seems released from the confines of optical logic, set free to light up anything and anywhere.

Blade Runner opens in a city of a thousand stars where fire blasts into the sky and the world is split, as it is in *Metropolis*, between the rich who reside in towers and the poor who exist on (or under) the ground. In the opening sequence LA's famous skyline is stretched and extended with fire and light, hovercrafts rocket past the camera, their ignited exhausts apparently causing circular optical flares on the camera's lens, as it too seems to hover in the night sky, gazing in awe at the visual feast before it. As if to acknowledge the spectacle, as well as the film's narrative focus on human replication and the workings of the soul, the camera cuts to show an extreme close-up of an eye, the bursts of fire and illumination from the flaming city reflecting on its translucent surface like a constellation of suns imploding beyond a watery horizon. Two vast metallic structures replicating Mayan pyramids thrust yet more stroboscopic light beams into the dark sky above, as the hovercraft moves close enough for the innumerable

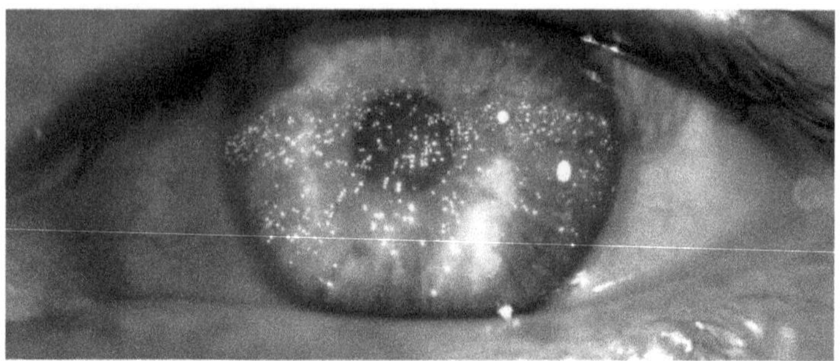

11   *Blade Runner.* Scott's city of the future is transformed into stars in the reflection of Deckard's (Harrison Ford) eye

windows on their angled surface to pulsate with heat and life. As Scott Bukatman has argued, Scott and Trumbull's luminous opening sequence 'is less the depiction of an object than the construction of an environment'.[7] An entire future world is created through sculpted variations in the dynamic opposition between darkness and light.

As the hovercraft continues its flight through the city, more details about the Los Angeles of 2019 are explored in light. Moving at a lower level, the hovercraft flies past giant illuminated billboard screens advertising Chinese products, Coca-Cola and old American airline PanAm. Later, a cut inside the spacecraft reveals that the internal echoes the external; all the controls inside the spaceship are constructed with flashing computer screens and dials of coloured light. Luminous patterns and shapes attached to the architecture twirl and shift on the screen and on the window of the hovercraft, reflecting off the faces of protagonist Deckard (Harrison Ford) and his associate sitting inside. Light forms the architecture of the city on multiple levels and from multiple sources, creating a layered world of communication and reference. Electric and synthetic light combines with the more natural qualities of starlight, merging notions of the modern and the archaic, the sacred and profane. This integration continues on the bustling street below where people walk around in the rain holding both old-fashioned Eastern umbrellas and styles with handles made from glowing fluorescent cylinders, an arresting mode of synthetic light that is replicated the first time we see Deckard as he sits reading a newspaper in front of a shop window packed full of televisions and neon tubes curved into patterns. The combination of pink and blue-green synthetic light with darkness and constant rain is distinctly dystopic, creating an uncertain atmosphere that is only emphasised by the binaries of old and new, poverty and wealth, starlight and streetlight.

Sumptuous illumination and the old–new dichotomy continue when Deckard visits his soon-to-be love interest Rachael inside one of the Mayan-shaped structures. Outside, the sun sits on the horizon either rising or setting amidst the gloom. The space beyond the techno-pyramids glows with a yellow haze from the combined luminosity of innumerable electric lights. This glow combines with that of the golden sun and pushes into the marbled room, glinting off the stone that flanks the walls and floor. As Rachael walks towards Deckard, the light shimmers and shifts as though reflecting off an unseen pool of water. This light has no perceivable source, so that the space becomes more reminiscent of the magical atmospheric interior of an Egyptian pyramid in which transformative acts of spiritual worship took place, than a clinical scientific location of twenty-first-century bio-engineering. Outside, vast human-made structures break the light, concentrating the sun's glare into cones of illumination. Dr Eldon Tyrell (Joe Turkell) asks Deckard to carry out a replicant test on Rachael. Deckard's complaint that 'it's too bright in here' is answered when Tyrell presses a button and an invisible shade moves down over the vast window, instantly altering the atmosphere inside the space and changing the colour of the key light from yellow to blue. In the gloom, using close analysis of the light in Rachael's eyes, Deckard realises that she is a replicant.

Whether inside or outside, amidst luxury or trash, in a reflection of *Blade Runner*'s narrative emphasis on memory and the nature of humanity, familiar nostalgia merges with strange futurism in densely lit sequences of opulent cinematic spectacle.

Just as the nature of Rachael's 'life' is revealed in *Blade Runner* via close scrutiny of the shifting quality of the light in her eyes, so too does light prove the existence of the Robot Hel's life force in *Metropolis*. Captured by Rotwang (Rudolf Klein-Rogge) and Fredersen (Alfred Abel), Maria (Brigitte Helm) is imprisoned in Rotwang's laboratory and put to sleep inside a cylindrical glass bed connected by wires to the robot Hel. Rotwang paces around the room flipping switches and checking gauges, constantly illuminating dials as he floods his equipment with electricity in preparation for his ground-breaking experiment. As he depresses the penultimate lever a silver orb above Maria's bed begins to glow and pulsate with energy. Placing his hands on the final handles Rotwang takes a deep breath before turning on the machine in a burst of action. Illumination twists and pulsates in strings of energy that look like lightening, making a connection on the screen between Maria and the orb with light. The camera cuts to show Hel's sleek, silver exterior, shining in the glow cast from circular rings of light that travel up and down her inanimate seated body, hinting at imminent transformation. The lightning bolts travelling between Maria's body and the orb intensify, filling the screen with vibrating pulses of electrified illumination. Around Hel, the Saturn-like rings incrementally increase in number and strength. Throughout Rotwang's laboratory liquid bubbles and equipment flashes, as the music builds suspense to a climactic crescendo over a wide shot of Maria and Hel, joined now by electricity, light and life. Finally, an illuminated heart in Hel's chest takes shape, flashing and spreading vein-like threads of light throughout her body, as though illumination is both her bloodstream and source of existence.

Metropolis's transformation sequence is a startling feat of cinematic spectacle that emphasises the power of extreme illumination as a tool of communication, metaphor and excitement. Günther Rittau (UFA's acknowledged intricate in-camera special-effects expert), discusses the difficulties involved in representing the Robot's metamorphosis:

> Electric currents tend to be invisible. On the other hand, the phantastic-mysterious transformation now taking place naturally had to be rendered in images. We illuminated liquids in strange test-tubes and made them bubble, the electric apparatus surrounding Maria was made to emit sparks and we gradually enveloped it in huge arcs of lightning, at the same time as rings of fire formed around the robot, moving up and down her body. As she became human, her blood circulation lit up. We spent months in the lab preparing these effects, with photo-chemistry playing a major role, as well as the most unlikely aids [such as] a silver ball, black velvet, liquid soap, vaseline, vignettes … Some strips of celluloid had to be exposed up to thirty times.[8]

Light in this context is used to both astound and to indicate the moment at which Hel becomes conscious, marking one of the first cinematic moments in which illumination communicates the sentience of the 'other'. Light has been used throughout cinematic history to prove that robots, aliens and otherwise inanimate objects are alive. It is the piercing red and yellow light of HAL's eye in *2001* that proves his existence and that is extinguished when he is 'killed'; a similar red eye shines out from *The Terminator*'s (James Cameron, 1984) metallic skull, fading to black as he 'dies' at the end of the film. In numerous science-fiction films, as will be discussed in the next section, from *Close Encounters* to *Aliens* (James Cameron, 1986) light is the means through which the spectator is encouraged to believe in the consciousness of a being from (or the existence of) another world. This connection between light and life – both the belief that things are working when the light is 'on' and the association of illumination with consciousness and existence – was formed in religious doctrine and emphasised for hundreds of years across science, art, culture and philosophy, from 'let there be light' via photosynthesis to *WALL.E* (Andrew Stanton, 2008). At the same time, it brings us back full circle to the discussion of the importance of cinematic 'eye light' in Chapter 1, as a means of forging both identity and a greater emotional connection – a greater level of belief – between character and spectator. When the lights are on, in the cinema at least, someone is definitely home.

Outer space

As much as the cinematic future is a place of floodlit cities and animate robots, it also offers an environment in which the existence of other worlds, alien life forms and extensive space travel becomes possible. Light in the cinema enables the creation of an imagined future in which giant spacecrafts transport humans on interstellar missions, where gleaming steel, blue strobes, flashing cockpits and weapons made of light announce the thrilling spectacle of time travel. At the same time, science-fiction cinema has embraced the creation of a magical alternative present in which luminous beings from outer space visit the earth, declaring both their arrival and their 'special' abilities in dramatic bursts of light and sound. In each case the desire to construct an 'out there', 'elsewhere' or 'other' is met with expressive lighting techniques that sculpt futuristic set designs and model alien bodies into believable, emotive, empathetic imaginary forms.

In *Close Encounters of the Third Kind*, a dramatic influx of illumination reported via luminous descriptions and arresting visual experiences announces the arrival of aliens on earth. In the Mexican desert after the mysterious discovery of a number of immaculate fighter planes that have been missing since 1945, an old man who witnessed their arrival tells scientists that 'the sun came out last night, and it sang.' Elsewhere, in an air traffic control centre in Indianapolis a radar screen emitting bright green computer light pinpoints an unidentified moving object. A pilot explains via radio what he can see to puzzled colleagues: 'To tell you the truth, it's odd and it's rather brilliant. It's the brightest pulse of light I've ever seen, alternating white to red. The colours are a little striking …Traffic is quite luminous.' On the same night, in Muncie, Indiana, Barry, a small boy, wakes when all his toys turn themselves on and light up. Downstairs the fridge has been raided and something luminous is moving around off-screen, making the little boy smile and laugh. Across town a sudden power outage means electrician Ray (Richard Dreyfuss) must leave his family and drive into the night in order to fix the problem. Already predisposed to the technical function of light due to his job (and his evocative name) Ray seems destined to witness expressive illumination. Alone on the open road, Ray stops to check his map. Behind him a car pulls up, its four lights – two white and two yellow – shine through the back window into the cab of the truck before he waves them past. When Ray stops again a few moments later by a railway crossing another car appears in the rear window. This time, however, instead of driving past Ray's truck when he waves them on, the car's six lights – four white, two orange – float upwards, revealing a bank of blue lights underneath the craft that Ray cannot see. Spielberg plays with the contrast between familiar and unfamiliar light and motion, teasing spectatorial anticipation. When a line of postboxes starts inexplicably shaking Ray knows something is wrong. Suddenly the radio and all the lights in Ray's cab switch off, just before an intense blue-white spotlight shines down on the cab from above. Smoke fills the screen, Ray panics and looks out of the cab at the sky above, only to be blinded and burned by the pulsating lights of the alien spaceship as it passes overhead. In each of these opening scenes, Spielberg and Trumbull suggest alien presence with references to, or arresting visions of, inexplicable coloured illumination. The awe of the characters in the film mirrors our own wide-eyed admiration of the images on the screen, aligning the light of transformative alien encounters with the luminous cinematic experience.

In *Close Encounters*, light marks the alien body and voices an alien language as much as it notes their arrival. The spaceships

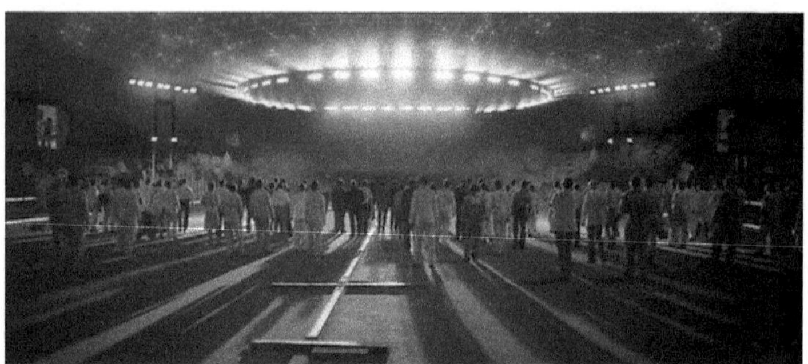

12 *Close Encounters of the Third Kind.* The luminous mother ship lands, flooding the screen with artificial light

themselves are almost entirely constructed with banks of coloured light that pulsate and scan in formation, while each craft has its own colour scheme and size, its own individuality. At the end of the film in the skies over Devil's Tower, as Ray and Jillian (Melinda Dillon) cling to the rocks above the landing station awaiting another alien encounter, the stars in the sky shift and create new constellations while shooting across the heavens, again emphasising, as in *Blade Runner*, a connection between the wonders of the natural world and the cinema; between some kind of innate 'natural' divinity and humanity's driven determination to use technology to understand, master and replicate this kind of spectacle.

Smaller alien crafts, their lights blazing in the form of features, swing over the tower, marking the way for the much larger mother-ship. Using a giant bank of rectangular coloured lights and a single tune the scientists begin to communicate with their visitors. This is only a preliminary exchange, however. When the mother ship arrives in a plume of electrified clouds, a scene of outstanding spectacle and outlandish illumination begins in which the entire frame is lit up with coloured lights so intense many of the scientists put on sunglasses. After communicating in a dazzling volley of pulses and noise, the mother ship opens its doors, flooding the scene with blinding white light and releasing Barry, along with many of the servicemen and civilians who'd been abducted from earth over the preceding years. As Roy M. Anker notes, at this point in the film

> Spielberg has slowly ratcheted up the 'wonder stakes' to the point of stupefaction at the sheer gloriousness of the spectacle that far outstrips any other screen evocation of the coming of the holy. It is the quintessential Spielberg stylistic signature in a film career that is filled with light … The splendour of the technology is so extreme and compelling that it assumes traits of the divine.[9]

Again, the link between excessive, inexplicable light and the creative power of filmmakers to control and shape it evokes a keen sense of religious fervour. After *Close Encounters* Spielberg continued to imagine aliens who communicate and heal with heavenly light creating *E.T. the Extra-Terrestrial*, whose index finger glows with the power to cure, understand and love. In these films we are encouraged to dream, imagine and have 'faith' in light, to control it, to reach up to the stars and draw them down from the sky, to believe in beings that are formed from and have the power to shape illumination, to be immersed in and impressed by a wondrous cinematic experience of overflowing optical intensity.

These films are the exception, however, not the rule, since cinematic outer space is rarely an environment of hopeful illumination, and is seldom inhabited by friendly aliens who use light as a positive force. It goes without saying that scenes of darkness, where light is absent and one cannot see, are commonly used for threatening effect. Without dark unfamiliar dangers, the unknown would be without drama, mystery or suspense. At the same time, as Mike O'Pray has suggested, in science-fiction horror films, light, especially blue light, continues to be used as code for both the as-yet-unseen alien 'other', the mysterious nature of outer space, and the uncontrollable incomprehensibility of artificial technological advance.[10] Seeping under doorways, filtering through spaceship windows, blinking up from control panels, this blue-white illumination combines the cold, hard, human-made qualities of steel with natural, eerie moonlight.

The opening of *Aliens* offers a particularly arresting example of this kind of icy illumination. From abstract blue lines of light in pitch-black darkness the word 'Aliens' forms on the screen, forging an immediate connection between this light and the alien itself, before the 'I' of the title stretches and expands, becoming whiter all the time like a hole being torn in the fabric of space, or the birth of a star, until stark white light consumes the screen, as though the aliens have taken over already. In the cockpit of Ripley's (Sigourney Weaver) spaceship blue light, apparently emanating from the nebula outside, filters through the windows. Everything glitters with decades of space dust, as if the ageing stars themselves have entered her cabin to mark the years she has spent in stasis. In her perspex life-support pod, Ripley lies like sleeping beauty, dappled in blue-grey light. Instead of a prince, however, a robotic scanner arrives to wake her, breaking through the craft in a shower of white sparks before emerging out of a fog of light that makes it momentarily unidentifiable, heightening suspense. Once the machine enters, scanning is indicated by the vertical line of blue light that tracks back and forth over the interior, cutting through the swirling smoke in the room, making diaphanous liquid patterns in the air.

In the hospital space station the light momentarily shifts: here it is cold, white and clinical. In one form or another, however, the blue light, the alien light, returns. In the boardroom scene it lies to the left and right of Ripley, streaming through the rectangular windows on either side of the room and in the edges of the strip lighting above her. Like her nightmares of becoming a living host, she cannot shake off the fear and sensation of the alien body. What is significant here is that the natural blue light of the nebula matches the electric blue light of the scanner and the key light of the rooms on the space station, along with the dominant blue aura earth seems to

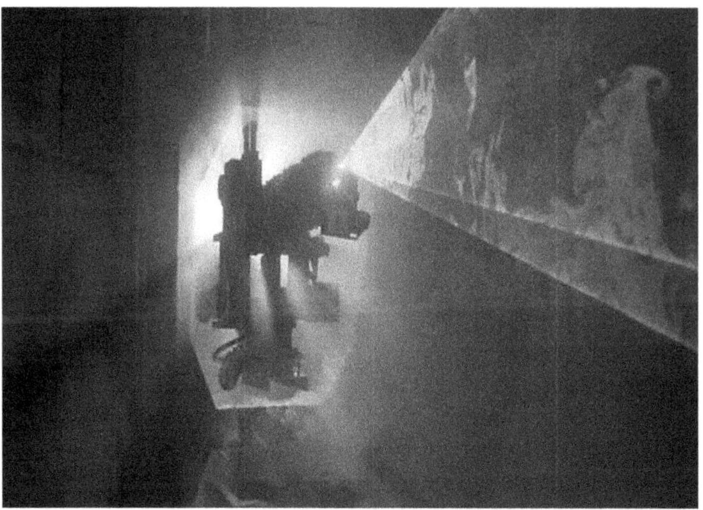

13   *Aliens*. A robotic scanner makes fluid light patterns in the smoke

emit when viewed from outer space. This light appears at once wholly artificial and entirely natural, connecting the alien, the mechanical and the human, suggesting, as the *Alien* films do in their depiction of the aliens as protective mothers, that the technological, biological and emotional boundary between 'us' and 'them' is more blurred than we might like to think.

Blue is not the only shade of illumination in space. The searching white lights of the torches used by the salvage team in Ripley's spaceship are almost as threatening as the strobe lights of the scanner. Here they recall the aggressive use of torchlight in *Metropolis* when Rotwang and Fredersen chase Maria through the depths of the workers' city. In Lang's film the beams seek Maria out, highlighting her terrified frame against the walls of the cavern, attacking her features, emphasising their alabaster shock, casting her shadow across the ground, ensnaring her image on the screen. As the torchlight in *Aliens* similarly flicks intrusively over the walls and equipment of Ripley's ship, finally seeking out her face behind perspex safety, its penetrating violence recalls the way light, inspired by directional torchlight, has been used as a more specific weapon in popular science fiction, from ray guns and laser beams in both versions of *War of the Worlds* (Byron Haskin, 1953 and Steven Spielberg, 2005) to light sabres in *Star Wars* (George Lucas, 1977–2005). These dangerous futuristic light weapons are inspired by electricity, science-fiction novels and the invention of the laser beam in 1960, as well as a fascination with the discovery of the extent of the electromagnetic spectrum from radio waves through visible light and ultraviolet to X-rays and gamma radiation. With their combination of evocative gunpowder sparks and electric lightning bolts, light weapons exemplify the way light on the screen can be sculpted with pinpoint accuracy and channelled for terrifying effect. Underground or in space, in darkness and gloom, torchlight and illuminated weapons become both a metaphor for uncovering the truth or seeking the unknown – a representation of the imaginative inquiring mind – and an aggressive tool of deadly power.[11] In these futuristic visions of earth or outer space, torches and lasers define and shape, swirling and shifting light across the screen, illuminating actors' faces and reconfiguring cinematic space, designating the field of vision, while reflexively replicating the triangular cone of the cinema projector. In this context cinematic light is at once vibrant, arresting and fatal.

Computer worlds

The invention of the personal computer in the mid-twentieth century, coupled with its now ubiquitous status as a permanent feature of modern life and its relative screen composition, offers the cinema a more recent and familiar alternative realm to imagine and represent. Computer games, parallel computer worlds and virtual lives have all been visualised on the screen in films that either transport characters inside programs or

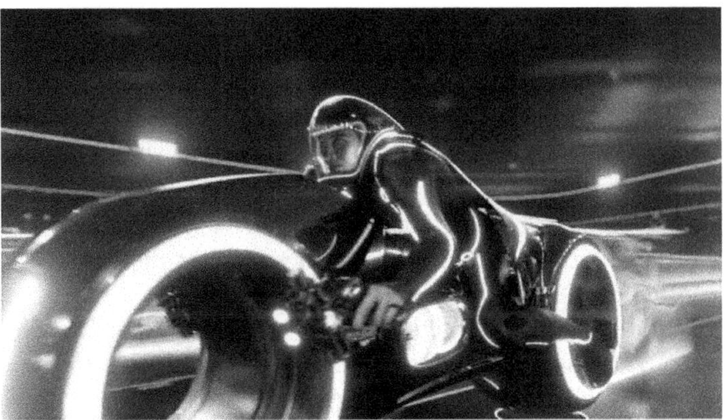

14   *TRON: Legacy*. Sam (Garrett Hedlund) on his light bike

depict the drama that unfolds when the world of the computer infiltrates 'real' life. In these situations expressive structural lighting techniques are used to authenticate the digital matrixes, circuits and data of a mainframe setting.

In *TRON: Legacy* (Joseph Kosinski), the 2010 reboot of the ground-breaking 1982 computer-world film, light is the architectural material of the digital realm: everything on-screen is constructed from spectacular fluorescent shapes sculpted into building, machine or human form. Although narratively simplistic, the film's cinematic value lies in its demonstration of computer light's creative cinematic potential. Awesome illumination reinvigorates two-dimensional characters and a clumsy script, recalling the similarly lacklustre narrative dynamism and outstanding digital light work of *Avatar* (James Cameron, 2009). When viewed in 3D the strange, dazzling beauty of a virtual world built entirely from artificial light assaults the eye with an almost unbearable intensity. Playing on the connection between velocity and illumination (although not actually able to travel at the speed of light) in *TRON* 's world of The Grid people ride curvaceous neon light bikes that leave lustrous solid tracks in their wake, while clad in colour-coded light suits (white for the good guys, orange for the bad) that turn humans into luminous armoured machines. Inside the computer game objects and people are not drawn, they are lit. The Grid, as program creator Kevin Flynn (Jeff Bridges) states, is 'a place of infinite possibility'. For all the awe-inspiring human-made light on offer in the virtual world, however, after existing entirely inside The Grid, all Quorra (Olivia Wilde) wants is to feel some real-world sunshine on her face. At the end of the film when Quorra and Sam (Garrett Hedlund) ride off into a quotidian sunrise together, the film suggests that however spectacular and infinite the digital realm might be, the lure of natural light in an imperfect world continues to prove irresistible.

Since the late 1990s, in a similar manner to the way cold blue light is used as a code for outer space, a synthetic green wash has become prevalent in films that seek to transport viewers inside the spectacular architecture or atmosphere of a binary digital environment, while questioning their utopian sensibilities. As a means of visually distancing the imaginary constructed world of *The Matrix* (Wachowski brothers, 1999) from the devastated 'natural' light of the 'real' world Neo (Keanu Reeves) chooses, acid-green tones permeate across the surface of the programmed scenes in the film, seeping onto skin, highlighting concrete buildings and motel signs, tingeing everything with a touch of acidity. The shade even infiltrates the *Warner Brothers* and *Village Roadshow Pictures* logos at the start of the film, suggesting a (now commonplace event-movie) synthesis between the filmic diegesis and the non-diegetic environment – between the computer and 'real' life. It is important to differentiate between green as a solid, painted colour or accent, and the way the shade washes across the screen in this instant, since here light itself is a nauseating colour, diffusing across every object and corner of Neo's virtual life. Joshua Clover discusses the way this pale-green-tinted light adds to a sense of individual entrapment and segregation:

Bodies may be in the same place, but nothing happens collectively; scene after scene is shot to emphasise the isolation of the individual. Green filtering creates a 'sickly' ambience (according to Bill Pope, the film's Director of Photography); the entire synthworld takes on a static, dead appearance that finds its apex in the fluorescent overheads of the Metacortex cubicle farm. This is only fitting; the optical manipulations of the lighting do the same work of separation as cubicle architecture itself.[12]

A lack of colour variation and an absence of yellow sunlight, combined with the virtual eradication of pinks and reds, ensure everyone in the alternative world of *The Matrix* looks ill, as though their environment is trying to communicate a sense of their enslaved situation as human batteries that power a world run by machines. Natural light, just like the 'real' world, no longer exists. The film suggests that its characters are trapped directly inside those electric coded green figures that buzz on Neo's clock radio and stream down the screen at the start of the film.

The green computer text to which *The Matrix* constantly returns embodies all that is artificial and uncertain about the digital world. As with the use of light in *Blade Runner*, this light is precariously balanced between nostalgia and futurism, since it recalls the green phosphors that were used on most computer displays in the 1970s and 1980s (the same green computer text that appears on radar screens in *Close Encounters* and that Ripley looks at on the space station in *Aliens*), while at the same time apprehensively hinting at the nightmarish possibilities of state-of-the-art computer technology. In *The Social Network* (2010) director David Fincher takes the connection between computers and an anxious yellow-green tone one stage further, eradicating the distinction between the world of computers and Mark Zuckerberg's (Jessie Eisenberg) reality. Harvard and Los Angeles, lecture halls and boardrooms: all are enveloped in a subtle green light that hints at the infiltration of computers, the internet, and their social networks into every area of our lives.

Depicting a similar, albeit slightly lighter shade of green than Fincher's earlier psychotic dystopia *Fight Club* (1999), *The Social Network* uses the diffusion of light through synthetic filters and digital post-production methods to imagine a tainted present in which everyone is becoming increasingly technologically dependent and less able to communicate on a human(e) level in the physical world.

Imag(in)ing emotion

The cinematic imagination does not only extend into the future, towards outer space, or inside computer networks with light. One of the primary values of the cinema as both an entertainment medium and an art form is its ability to travel within, to visualise the workings of the human mind, to imagine thought processes and emotions on the screen. As much as light invents and authenticates unfamiliar environments, it also makes familiar feelings spectacular. Expressive illumination can remove the spectator from a character's humdrum external reality and transport us inside their head, flashing coloured psychic reactions and spontaneous memories across the screen. These moments of luminous revelation occur most frequently at the height of emotional experience, as though bodies can no longer contain the intensity, bursting in coloured waves of illuminated expression.

It is the sheer breadth of lighting styles, colours and directions during the fantasy ballet sequence of *An American in Paris* (1951) that evokes Jerry Mulligan's (Gene Kelly) mixed-up emotional state. Lise (Leslie Caron) has left Jerry for another man. As Jerry sits alone on a balcony at a black-and-white ball, he is overwhelmed by feelings of loss and love. Shot by cinematographer John Alton, shadows begin to dance on Jerry's back and face and wind blows across the scene, rejoining the edges of his torn drawing before he imagines stepping into it and the fantasy sequence begins. Although for much of the ballet 'movie lighting' still applies, when the couple dance around a fountain, suddenly the mood darkens, torchlight chases Jerry and the lighting becomes psychedelic, flashing green and red in line with Jerry's reverberating heart. Towards the end of the sequence, Jerry swings Lise into his arms and they dance seductively in front of a heavily backlit screen, transforming into shadows in the yellow glow. The lighting shifts from yellow to blue to red to blue to white and red again, as they drape intimately around the fountain and each other in the diffused light. Chiming with Jerry's emotional state, the lighting in this part of the ballet is frenzied, uncontained and joyous. Here Angela Dalle Vacche discusses the critical reception of the sequence at the time of the film's release:

> Critics noted that its excessive length (seventeen minutes) and cost ($450,000) appear to be marks of exaggeration. The pace is invariably described as 'frantic', and the fireworks like bursting of colours as 'delirious'. The intensity of the ballet's emotional and visual impact on the viewer is also remarked upon. All these excessive features point to Minnelli's surrealistic insight that the artist can transfigure what is imaginary into a reality more compelling and more real than the real world itself.[13]

The sequence and the critical reaction are suggestive of the power of illumination, when combined with colour, movement and set, to communicate, and most importantly, make real, alternative states of feeling and heightened emotions, reconfiguring staged sets into the believable landscapes of Jerry's mind. As with colour, lighting's status as a malleable cinematic tool enables infinite creative variation, atmosphere and emotive potential within a single location.

An ability to offer immediate shifts in tone, mood and setting within the same scene means that as much as light is used to communicate intense emotion, it also frequently figures as an indication that a character is experiencing the sudden involuntary pull of a significant memory. I have already mentioned the way torchlight is often used to indicate the penetrating functions of an inquisitive mind. Similarly in *Eternal Sunshine of the Spotless Mind* (Michel Gondry, 2004) torches and spotlights are used to represent Joel's (Jim Carrey) memories as he attempts to prevent them from being ripped away. The film can be understood as a love story in reverse. When Joel discovers that his ex-girlfriend Clementine (Kate Winslet), unable to cope with their devastating break-up, has had him erased from her mind by a mysterious company that has developed the technology to obliterate unwanted memories, he decides to have the same procedure. During the process Joel realises however, that along with his bad memories of Clementine, he will also lose the good ones, so he tries to hide Clementine from the technicians and machines by taking her deep within his mind to memories in which she doesn't belong. In the film expressive lighting is used both optimistically and confrontationally, at times illuminating and therefore saving the spaces Joel loves, at others seeking the couple out and aggressively tracking their movements. The more intense Joel's experience of forgetting, the more he attempts to hide and thus retain his memories of Clementine, the darker and more theatrically lit the image becomes. As Ellen Kuras, the film's cinematographer recalls in an interview with John Pavlus, Michel Gondry had a very clear idea of the kind of lighting he wanted for these sections of the film:

> As Joel burrows deeper into his own memories in a vain attempt to hide Clementine from the Lacuna technicians, the scenes' quality of light becomes distinctly dramatic. 'We didn't want to make it a huge departure from the film's look, but we wanted to signal to the audience that we were in the tunnel of the mind', Kuras explains. 'Michel's visual analogy, which was brilliant, was inspired by the French film *Le Boucher*: a car is driving on a deserted country road at night, and you can only see what's illuminated by the throw of the headlights. When you're remembering something, you don't get a full picture; you only see certain glimpses of the scene in your head, depending on what

you're focusing on. So, for our 'memory light', we attached a single clip light on top of the camera for closer shots; we used a Par can to similar effect in the wide shots.[14]

Kuras's 'memory light' is used to optimum effect at the end of the film when almost all of Joel's memories of Clementine have been erased. The film returns to Montauk, to the beach where Joel and Clementine first met. In the darkness they run along the shoreline together until they come to an abandoned house and break inside. In a gesture that is weighted with symbolism Clementine picks up a torch from the sideboard and starts using it to light their way. She is now in control of the light, and thus also seems to be attempting to manipulate the direction of Joel's thoughts and his ability to retain his past. As it flits around the crumbling beach house, isolating their faces and shrinking the world, Clementine's searchlight in the dark works as a metaphor for a mind that is hunting for lost memories. In *Eternal Sunshine*, light is used as a sculptural visual tool and a symbol of the process of remembrance, literally depicting the way we either purposefully or involuntarily seek out past experiences until they are illuminated amidst the darkness of the rest of our thoughts.

In *Three Colours: Blue* (1993), the memory of Julie's loss (Juliette Binoche) as she desperately tries to recover from the aftermath of a horrific car crash in which her composer husband and young daughter were killed, surges out of her mind and onto the screen. Here, instead of the isolated, directional illumination of Joel's 'memory light', Julie's past and present loss floods the screen in pulses of colour-coded agony. Julie is convalescing in a building surrounded by trees and lined with balconies. At the end of each floor is a glass screen that lets through dappled sunlight onto the terraces. Each screen in the building is made of clear glass except Julie's, on the bottom left-hand side, which glows with a vibrant, intense blue as sunlight streams through it. As she reclines in a chair, resting or sleeping with her eyes closed, the natural, almost imperceptible light on her face is suddenly replaced with a blast of blue illumination, and simultaneously she wakes, startled by the memory of the sound of her husband's final unfinished 'European concerto'. The blue light is strong and excessive, it fills the screen with colour washing across the frame and Julie's shocked face as the anguish she has been trying to suppress suddenly forces its way to the surface of her thoughts. As Marek Haltof has pointed out, the terrible trauma and intensity of remembering and reliving loss when imagined with a combination of arresting light and dramatic music, works to 'emphasise the importance of memory'.[15] These arresting moments of excruciating illumination are often followed by short periods during which the screen goes entirely black, as though Julie's emotions have become so intense and the coloured lighting so vibrant that the screen has been overloaded, short-circuited by too much power: too painful for representation.

Like a bomb or explosion, the centre of which is too bright to perceive, when a character is pushed to the edge of emotional sensation through drug use, insanity or transformative spiritual experience, cinematic light fluctuates and burns with spectacular power. As in *Blue*, intense and unpredictable feelings necessitate extreme and erratic optical effects. When Scottie (Jimmy Stewart) loses his mind over Madeleine (Kim Novak) in *Vertigo* (Alfred Hitchcock, 1958) his nightmare anticipates his subsequent decent into manipulative madness in coloured light, flashing from purple to green to orange to red, until he imagines falling from the tower as a silhouette into a bottomless rectangle of searing white space. Similarly, in Kubrick's seminal work of luminous wonder, *2001: A Space Odyssey*, as Bowman (Keir Dullea) thunders through time in the awe-inspiring star-gate sequence, space itself seems to split apart with rays of coloured light that reflect his transcendental experience. Neon illumination cascades in front of Bowman's flickering eye, his face appearing momentarily in freeze-frame, as though petrified by the luminosity of the bursting stars, expanding galaxies and multicoloured landscapes that surround him. Technology and irrepressible emotional experience combine at the apex of cinematic purpose. As Scott Bukatman explains, 'Through slitscan technologies, Trumbull created a set of images that were little more than organised patterns of light – the very stuff of cinema.'[16]

Danny Boyle evokes Kubrick's psychological concern and luminous aesthetic in *Sunshine* (2007), a film in which light itself is the drug, the cause, and the representation of insanity for astrophysicists who must explode a nuclear bomb at the centre of the sun in order to resurrect it as a new star. As characters go insane from excessive sun exposure, the film uses jump-cuts and temporal distortion, along with overwhelming flashes of computer-generated light to hide monstrous character Pinbacker (Mark Strong) from view, so that we only see fragments and hints of his sun-damaged body. In these moments excessive digital light becomes as suspenseful and deceptive as darkness, bleaching out meaning and making the image almost indecipherable. In many ways *Sunshine* exemplifies the way imaginative cinematic light, anticipated by the star-gate sequence of *2001*, reaches its pinnacle through computer generation. Via digital special effects, malleable lighting techniques are pushed to their limits as space is not just moulded with light by the cinematographer, but created anew by the online technician. The computer transforms cinema's relationship with the real, one of the key signifiers of which is the way both natural and electric light bounces off people and objects, leaving a trace of their existence in reality. To an extent, in a contemporary digital context, the presence in an image of either naturalistic or electric lighting no longer necessitates the actual presence of that light on location or on the set. Light need not literally exist in either time or space anymore – it can shine anywhere, it can light up anything or anyone. However, the association of light and the natural continues, since within such a malleable contemporary context, highlighting computer-generated images with constructed digital light is one of the key means through which the object, set or character is made to look more realistic – light and shade make the image three-dimensional and in so doing they authenticate the imagined worlds on-screen. The sheer range and variation of light that the computer affords means that the filmmaker is unencumbered by more traditional lighting restrictions associated with availability and source. As a result, lighting becomes an even greater creative and experimental tool through which the filmmaker can bend and shape temporal experience, communicating intense emotion and constructing entirely imaginary environments. In *Sunshine*'s final moments, when protagonist Capa (Cillian Murphy) explodes his bomb and is literally absorbed at the moment of death in reverential slow motion by the overwhelming light of a supernova, Boyle attempts (as Kubrick did with his glowing star child in *2001*) to engage directly with our eternal fascination with illumination, with its ability to imagine and sculpt time and space, and with the fact that ultimately, just like the cinema itself, we are all at once agents and objects of light. As Anna Powell explains:

> Light physically permeates us in its passage through our (semi-transparent) bodies. It enters our brain cells by the transmutation of light waves into electrical charges by optic nerves. In a biological sense, then, we see nothing *but* light. Of seminal philosophical significance, we also *think* in images of light.[17]

Notes

1 Fritz Lang, quoted in T. Elsaesser, *Metropolis, BFI Film Classic* (London: BFI, 2000), p. 9. Elsaesser underlines the fact that Lang's emphasis of his vision of the Manhattan skyline from the deck of the *SS Deutschland* as the initial inspiration for the city in *Metropolis* is a myth since alternative evidence suggests that Lang, his producer Erich Pommer and his wife scriptwriter Thea von Harbou had already been discussing a film called Metropolis for over a year prior to the docking of the ship in New York.

2 T. Gunning, 'Lunar Illuminations', in J. Geiger and R. L. Rutsky (eds), *Film Analysis: A Norton Reader* (New York and London: Norton, 2005), pp. 64–81, p. 65.

3 G. King and T. Krzywinska, *Science Fiction Cinema: From Outerspace to Cyberspace* (London: Wallflower, 2000), p. 64.

4 Thea von Harbou quoted in W. Jacobsen and W. Sudendorf, *Metropolis: A Cinematic Laboratory for Modern Architecture* (Stuttgart/London: Edition Axel Menges, 2000), p. 9.

5 *Ibid.*, p. 23.

6 See S. Bukatman, 'The Artificial Infinite: On Special Effects and the Sublime', in A. Kuhn (ed), *Alien Zone II: The Spaces of Science Fiction Cinema* (London and New York: Verso, 1999), pp. 249–75, p. 250.

7 *Ibid.*, p. 259.

8 Günther Rittau quoted in Elsaesser, *Metropolis*, p. 25.

9 R. M. Anker, *Catching Light: Looking for God in the Movies* (Michigan and Cambridge: Eerdmans, 2004), pp. 286–7.

10 See O'Pray, *Film, Form and Phantasy*, p. 198.

11 See King and Krzywinska, *Science Fiction Cinema*, p. 81.

12 J. Clover, *The Matrix, BFI Modern Classic* (London: BFI, 2004), p. 67.

13 A. Dalle Vacche, *Cinema and Painting: How Art Is Used in Film* (Austin: University of Texas Press, 1996), p. 22.

14 J. Pavlus, 'Forget Me Not', *American Cinematographer*, 85(4) (April 2004), 36–47, 42.

15 M. Haltof, *The Cinema of Krzysztof Kieslowśki: Variations on Destiny and Chance* (London: Wallflower, 2004), p. 130.

16 Bukatman, 'Artificial Infinite', p. 264.

17 A. Powell, *Deleuze, Altered States and Film* (Edinburgh: Edinburgh University Press, 2007), p. 88.

II The absence of light

4   Mystery

> Where there is no light, one cannot see; and when one cannot see, his imagination starts to run wild.
>
> (John Alton, *Painting with Light*, [1949] 1995)

> Now it's dark.
>
> (Frank Booth (Dennis Hopper), *Blue Velvet*)

Nothing terrible has ever happened to me in the dark, yet I continue to be afraid of it. On a winter's evening, approaching the black space beneath a broken street light, my heart beats faster. Nerves tingle. My eyes strain to see into the void so that I might anticipate any violence from within. In order to walk forward I remind myself of all the times I have been safe in the dark before, soothing an overactive imagination so I can reach the safety of illumination on the other side. My fear feels instinctive, involuntary and primal. Compounded and encouraged by centuries of art and culture that forge a connection between darkness and danger, something at my core remains certain that bad things only happen at night. At the same time darkness is intriguing. It offers a blank space onto which our dreams and fears can project, an intimate gap between supposition and certainty that encourages imaginative exposition. The cinema is similarly convinced. Throughout its history, across genres and continents, darkness remains visual shorthand for secrecy and magic, anxiety and terror. As the cinematographer John Alton notes above, without light the imagination goes into overdrive, one 'begins to suspect that something is about to happen. In the dark there is mystery.'[1]

Part I of this book explained how expressive cinematic illumination helps us to sympathise, desire and understand the identity of complex protagonists, sculpting star infatuations. In films that seek to replicate the natural light of the real world, the passage of the sun and its accordant emotive indications of hope and despair are mirrored by protagonists in cinematic environments that rely on location architecture to mould authentic illumination into the spectacular shapes of emotional experience. Exterior and interior alternative worlds are imagined in explosions of awesome artificial light and colour that carve futuristic alien forms and landscapes, authenticating imaginary environments and visualising extreme sensation. And yet, these moments of arresting illumination often only stand out as such because of the darkness that surrounds and counterbalances them. Contrast and comparison is everything. A bursting firework is far more brilliant at night than during the day. The luminous glow of the cinema screen is all the more spectacular when viewed against the backdrop of a darkened auditorium. Light is inextricably connected and can only be fully understood in relation to its dark counterpart. As such, this chapter and the following two take *Film Light* towards its moody other side, charting a lack of illumination in the cinema. Just as light's presence has forged the identity, reality and imagination of characters across the history of cinema, so too has its absence. In the films discussed in this chapter, chiaroscuro and expressive lighting techniques limit the use of light to create suspense, threatening atmospheres and ambivalent protagonists. In these contexts cinematic darkness often connotes interiority: that which remains hidden, that which we cannot see. As much as illumination built imaginary worlds in the previous chapter, in this one, darkness offers a blank black space onto which our imaginations can project. In most cases, an absence of visual information results in an anxious or fearful response. When the sun wanes and grows dim on the cinema screen, when candles are lit and lamps flicker into life, when dusk falls into night, characters appear suspicious, facts seem indecipherable and atmospheres become mysterious. In these situations shadows, smoke and hiding places both protect and disguise, putting existence under threat, causing tension or terror, and harbouring confused, morally ambiguous characters who at once seek out, yet remain afraid of, the dark.

The films in this chapter, including *Double Indemnity* (Billy Wilder, 1944), *Once Upon a Time in the West* (Sergio Leone, 1968) and *The Blair Witch Project* (Daniel Myrick and Eduardo Sánchez, 1999) will be discussed somewhat outside their assumed positions as noirs, westerns or horrors. Certainly these generic definitions can be useful in thinking about the way light has been used across each of these categories, and much has been written on, for example, the association between the stark chiaroscuro conditions of German Expressionism and some film noirs, the connection between the hot noon-day sun of the open prairie and the western, or the link between darkness and a fear of the unknown in most horror films. However, I want to look at the way darkness is used expressively and themat- ically to communicate particular atmospheres and illuminate character identity across film genres, categories and cycles. Just as light is used to expansive and varied aesthetic ends, so too does its absence offer multiple emotive connotations. As Daniel Frampton has noted, in the cinema 'Darkness offers its own multitude of thoughts.'[2] Shadows and silhouettes; mist, fog and smoke; wardrobes, tunnels and caves; pitch-black voids; all offer different kinds of cinematic obscurity and oblivion that encourage distinct reactions and sensations. Darkness, or rather the sparse use of intense light to create stark shadows and bottomless holes of cinematic space, must be split into its constituent parts so that we might understand its representation and cinematic function more clearly, so that we might learn to see in the dark and walk through it.

Shadows and silhouettes

In the cinema the interdependent relationship between darkness and illumination is most clearly visualised when lighting becomes sparse and intense, creating stark shadows and black silhouettes that can be understood as external manifestations of internal processes. As the director Joseph von Sternberg has noted, the creation of shadows is dependent on the availability of appropriate light sources. Darkness in this context only exists via illumination. 'Each light furnishes its own shadow, and where we see a shadow we know there must be a light.'[3] At the same time, the purposeful use of shadows via framing, size and strength has become a key method of expression in the cinema, transferring the feelings and inner experiences of characters onto the screen at key narrative moments.

Historically, expressive shadows and silhouettes have appeared most frequently in, and are thus directly associated with, the horror genre and film noir. Suspicion and terror thrive in the dark. The appearance of shadows in each of these modes was originally thought to have been directly inspired by the oblique angles and nightmarish visions of 1920s German Expressionism, by films such as *Nosferatu* (F. W. Murnau, 1922) and *The Cabinet of Dr. Caligari* (*Das Cabinet des Dr. Caligari*, Robert Weine, 1920). However, although these films have certainly been influential generally, their specific use of a cast shadow to induce suspense and fear can also be seen concurrently in Hollywood films of the same era. As Patrick Keating has argued, although *Nosferatu* wasn't released in the USA until 1929, Harold Lloyd's 1920 film *Haunted Spooks* contains an almost identical cast shadow, suggesting that 'Cinematographers did not need to turn to German Expressionism to learn to associate shadows with crime and horror; they could simply turn to long-standing traditions in domestic culture.'[4]

Film noir definitions and aesthetics are bound up in similar shadow myths. In the 1960s and 1970s, film noir was used to describe a thematic and aesthetically similar cycle of thrillers spanning from John Huston's *The Maltese Falcon* in 1941 to Orson Welles's *Touch of Evil* in 1958.[5] Regarding illumination, these films were characterised by low-key, harsh contrasts: bright pools of light created ominous areas of darkness. Corrupt cops and femme fatales languished in gloomy rooms, trapped or hiding amidst the shadows cast from horizontal blinds and vertical staircases. Film noir lighting was defined against 'high-key' glamour or movie lighting. Much like the low-budget traditions of the horror genre, the limited budgets of film noirs, often classed as B-movies and made during the restrained film production era of the Second World War, encouraged cinematographers to experiment with reduced means, heightening tension with isolated key lights in confined sets.[6] Dramatic and overt, reflecting the dark psychology of its protagonists, film noir style was the opposite of 'invisible'. Like the chiaroscuro depths of Rembrandt or Caravaggio, noir appeared aggressively artistic, linking the stark dichotomy of light and shade to the murky morality of the underworlds in which it was set, tugging film towards art via overt stylisation. In film studies, for many years, writing on film noir was one of the only areas in which lighting aesthetics were discussed at length, since the striking illumination and aesthetic style of many noirs was seen to directly mirror their narrative content: dark palettes echoed the dark emotions and actions of their characters, offering multiple avenues for aesthetic investigation. More recently, however, critics have noted the difficulty in defining a mode that spans melodrama, thrillers, romance and war films and that was actually shot almost as much in high-key movie lighting as low-key chiaroscuro.[7] Not all noirs were black and many cinematographers had already been using these kinds of techniques to light Hollywood melodramas.[8] The dark and varied influences upon the horror genre and the aesthetic and generic instability of film noir suggest that any discussion of cinematic shadows benefits from a wider investigation of their use, position and impact across art and literature, while the interrogation of their appearance must reject generalisation and employ textual analysis on a case-by-case basis. To understand why shadows in the cinema are so frequently used to connote mystery, fear and suspicion, it is important to try to understand their wider cultural significance.

Although differing in the way they are cast, projected or attached, cinematic shadows can be loosely divided into two categories: those that are static and those that move or, rather, those produced by lighting objects and those connected to individuals. Static shadows divide and shape space, directing the eye away from areas of darkness towards illuminated faces and objects in an echo of the way dark chiaroscuro functions in the work of the late Renaissance painters, creating areas of light on the screen around which characters gather as if repelled by the encroaching black space that surrounds them. At the same time static shadows announce their own presence and significance in the way they emerge via light either cast or obstructed by the set itself, frequently evoking entrapment or deception via shadowed bars and concealed eyes. In *The Dark Corner* (Henry Hathaway, 1946), for example, the iconography of Bradford Galt's (Mark Stevens) private investigator's office, from horizontal window blinds that slice space into slits of light and shade, to the shadows cast by his own name on the walls of the room, create an atmosphere of self-interest and claustrophobia that emphasises his position as a down-on-his-luck recently released ex-con who is being tailed by persons unknown. In the absence of actual prison bars, cinema recreates them with stark lines of solidified shadow.

Of greater interest here, however, are those shadows that move: those that are connected to or evoke the human form. The history of the humanoid shadow emerges out of the ancient world in two iconic motifs that are each, much like our own, simultaneously connected to and separate from, the body and the self. In Ancient Egypt, as early as 2500 BCE, in hieroglyphs on the walls of pharaonic tombs depicting prayers and incantations that were supposed to help the deceased in the afterlife, *The Pyramid Texts* mention the 'Khaibit' as a darker aspect or reflection of the soul in shadow form.[9] Over a thousand years later in Homer's work *The Odyssey, c.*1000 BCE, Odysseus has a meeting with the shade or shadow of Achilles – his 'Atcta' – in the underworld.[10] On the one hand, there is the shadow as a representation of the soul or ego, as though a part of a person's being has cleaved away from the whole, appearing outside their physical body. On the other hand, emerging out of this idea is the concept of the shadow as a manifestation of a person after death or, in an alternative realm, revealing itself in the form of a ghost, spectre or ghoul. Since its inception, and perhaps as a result of its ontological status as a Platonic, cave-like medium of illumination and shadows, the cinema has embraced these dark metaphors of ancient history, returning time and again to the humanoid shadow as a visual representation of both the divided soul and the terrifying monster.

In *Nosferatu* shadows are synonymous with mystery and fear. In a section that begins with an intertitle that states: 'The ghostly evening light again seemed to revive the shadows of the castle', and in which Hutter reads the words 'Beware so that his shadow cannot burden your sleep with horrible nightmares', Count Orlok transforms into Nosferatu and drinks Hutter's blood as a shadow. As Victor I. Stoichita has discussed, indoors at night, cast from the light of a single candle or isolated lamp, shadows shrug off sunlit daytime sensibilities of limited size and expand to horrifying, unearthly proportion: 'the enormity of the shadows goes hand in hand with their demonization'.[11] As Nosferatu's shadow creeps up Hutter's terrified shrinking body, his features are wiped out and he becomes a claw-fingered, razor-eared symbol of unstoppable evil. Here the magnified humanoid shadow is anything but human. Swollen by isolated illumination and disconnected from the body by framing, his shadow seems enabled with occult power, operating outside its host like a dark extension of the mind. At the end of the film when Nosferatu hunts down Ellen in her bed, it is his shadow that sneaks up the staircase, his shadow that reaches out and clutches at her heart. Light and shade at once

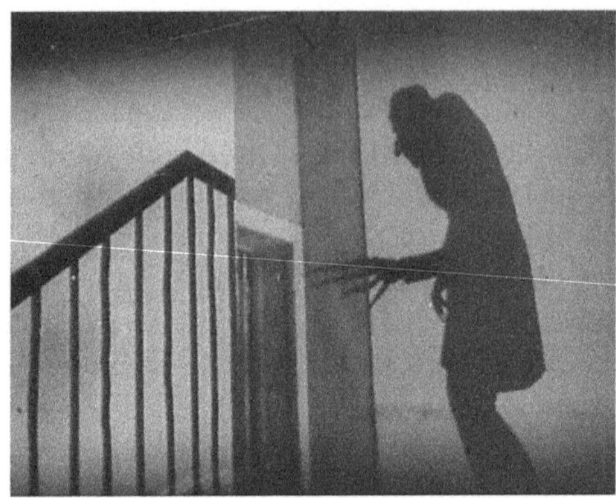

15 *Nosferatu/Nosferatu, eine Symphonie des Grauens.* Count Orlok's (Max Schreck) hideous shadow creeps towards his victim's door

construct a monster and an indication of presence: a suggestion of imminent danger and a vehicle of cinematic suspense.

Shadows indicate absence as much as they connote presence. They are traces of us but they are also figured as uncanny, at once embodied and disembodied, simultaneously proving existence and suggesting partial representation. In this context, the moment when the shadow separates from its referent entirely is perhaps more unnatural and terrifying than the shadow itself. As Mary Longstreet (Loretta Young) intimates in her description of a dream in *The Stranger* (Orson Welles, 1946): 'I've never had a dream like that before, it frightened me. The little man was walking all by himself across a deserted city square. Wherever he moved he threw a shadow. But when he moved away, Charles, the shadow stayed there behind him and spread out just like a carpet.' In this instance the shadow of the little man, killed by Mary's husband, school professor Charles (Orson Welles), in order to protect his secret identity as a wanted Nazi, operates as a metaphor for the little man's reverberating impact on the town, an impact that eventually leads to Mary's insanity and Charles's death.

In the 1970s the psychoanalyst Otto Rank suggested that the uncanny double or *Doppelgänger* had been regularly depicted as a shadow or mirror image, and that the fear arising from the representation of the other as a shadow was directly connected to anxieties about the self. Rank traced the origins of the shadow and its association with the soul across decades and continents from New Year's Eve shadow games that predict when someone will die in Germany and Austria, to the belief that it is unlucky to walk on your own shadow in Dutch New Guinea, since it is tantamount to stepping on your own spirit.[12] Rank's conviction that the shadow 'is clearly an independent and visible cleavage of the ego' is visualised regularly in the cinema, in films that emphasise psychic disruption and mental turmoil.[13] Moments after Walter Neff (Fred MacMurray) decides to kill his lover's (Phyllis Dietrichson (Barbara Stanwyck)) husband for the insurance money in *Double Indemnity*, he walks across a sparsely lit apartment towards floral curtains, smoking and thinking. Pausing momentarily before the full-length window, Walter's shadow is cast life-size on the fabric in front of him as the music surges and he reaches forward, tearing the curtains, and himself, apart. The split shadow predicts the physical and psychological impact of his murderous decision. Similarly, towards the end of *Bigger than Life* (Nicholas Ray, 1956) when Ed Avery's (James Mason) mania has reached almost total psychosis, both he and his shadow loom above his son as he forces him to do equations over and over again. Centrally framed, enormous and literally overbearing, the shadow embodies all that Ed has become, as though his madness has projected onto the walls of the living room in a graphic approx-imation of overwhelming mental distress. When his wife Lou (Barbara Rush) enters the room, Ed's shadow dominates the space between them, reflecting the drug-induced insanity that is forcing them apart. In each instance, shadows are used as the visual language of the unconscious, reflecting psychic disruption during moments of extreme emotion, marking the screen with the essence of a dark soul in turmoil.

Although silhouettes function in a comparative way to shadows, they are not the same. They share an interstitial position, as Emma Rutherford has noted, 'A silhouette is both something and nothing, a negative and a positive.'[14] And yet, while shadows duplicate the body, silhouettes turn people themselves into featureless shadows, concealing personal identification. Strong backlighting and the eradication of frontal key or fill illumination transforms those blocking the light into one-dimensional graphic forms. Used behind frosted glass to evoke mysterious strangers in multiple noirs, they are also employed to suggest the Everyman, the individual as an emblem, and the eternal continuation of narrative at the end of a film. In front of sunlit doorways and windows, especially in the western, bright vistas turn bodies into shapes, erasing individuality and marking men out as icons of the frontier. At the beginning of *Once Upon a Time in the West*, as Frank's gang wait for the train carrying Harmonica (Charles Bronson), Leone splits the frame apart with off-kilter wooden doorways in which the men lean in silhouette, faces hidden by the shadows from their hats, their leather duster coats flapping in the breeze. Later when Frank (Henry Fonda) enters the town saloon for a verbal confrontation with Harmonica, he pauses before pushing through the swing door, his Stetson hat, head and torso framed in silhouette by the doorway and the sunlight beyond, immortalising him in an iconic western moment. The instant recalls John Wayne's lumbering silhouette, hovering in a doorway between the homestead and the frontier at the end of *The Searchers* (John Ford, 1956) lacking a definitive place to belong in this rapidly transforming landscape. In its pure, simplistic, solid form, the silhouette emphasises the mythic status of these bad and good men, each one offering a different side of the American West, each one as sturdy, resolute and indefatigable as their black forms suggest.

In *Night of the Hunter* (Charles Laughton, 1955) the crude, simplistic form of the silhouette is emphasised to suggest a naive, childlike vision of terror. The first time John and Pearl

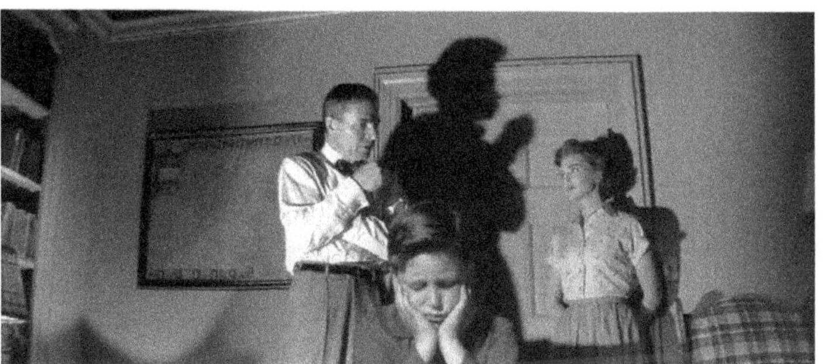

16 *Bigger Than Life*. The shadow representation of Ed Avery's (James Mason) insanity intrudes on family life

see the murderous preacher Harry Powell (Robert Mitchum) is as a shadow on the wall of their bedroom; his featureless dark head and hat suddenly obliterate John's tiny form as he tells his sister Pearl a story. This moment marks the way John can see the black nature of Henry's soul, while many of the adults in the village cannot. After Harry murders their mother, the children go on the run in a small boat, paddling down river as fast as they can during the day and sleeping on it at night. Exhausted and filthy, one night they come across some barns in which John decides they must sleep. From the river, the buildings look like cardboard cut-outs, looming black silhouettes that recall childlike drawings, while in a strongly backlit window a bird cage is visible in silhouette, reflecting the idealised, uncomplicated nature of John and Pearl's imagination. Waking at dawn, John hears a dog barking and the sound of Harry singing, before the murderous false prophet appears on the horizon in silhouette; an unstoppable superhuman force; a black stain on the landscape that the children might never escape. Later in the film, their salvation comes, however, in the form of an equally resolute gun-toting silhouette, that of Rachel Cooper (Lillian Gish) fearlessly protecting John and Pearl along with her adopted children through the night in a rocking chair cradling a shotgun, while Harry stalks outside. As in the

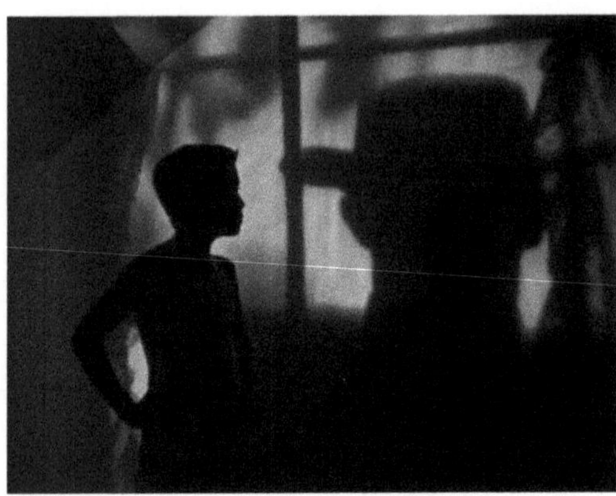

17   *The Night of the Hunter.* Harry Powell's (Robert Mitchum) shadow precedes his arrival, terrifying John's (Billy Chapin) silhouette

westerns mentioned above, the archetypes of good and evil – the protective mother and the murderous villain – confront each other as emblems; their depiction as graphic silhouettes operating as a forceful childlike visualisation of those eternal opposites that mark Harry's knuckles: love and hate.

Solid light

When mist, fog or smoke appears on the cinema screen, illumination solidifies, transformed into a substance almost as intangible and impenetrable as darkness. Clouds of grey light curl out of mouths and swirl beneath doorways, blurring space and making it difficult to see clearly, emphasising mystery and deception; encouraging imaginative investigation. Light clings to the shifting sculptural mass as though it has become an integral element of such strange weather phenomena, thickening an image that in turn deceives the eye. Used like static shadows to hide and disguise, mist, fog and smoke

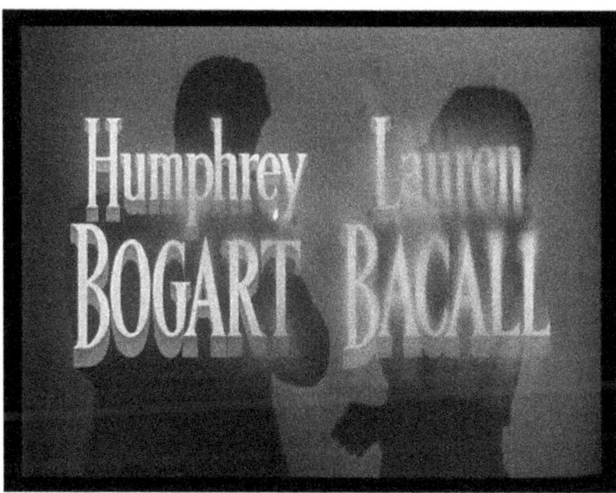

18   *The Big Sleep*. Lauren Bacall's title drifts seductively across the screen

also frequently turns characters into silhouettes, once again enabling iconic representation, while at the same time, each mode of solid light seeks and initiates a distinct emotional response from smoky nostalgia and fear amidst fog to the uncertain haze of elusive encounters in the mist.

The title sequence of *The Big Sleep* (Howard Hawks, 1946) opens with the silhouette of a man lighting a woman's cigarette behind a semi-transparent second frame. As the names of the film's stars – Humphrey Bogart and Lauren Bacall – appear on the screen side by side in front of the figures, the suggestion is clear that these are *their* bodies, joined and made iconic in the frame by shadow and position. The smoking silhouettes recall Bogart and Bacall's star personas, at once solid and mysterious, beautiful and intangible, seducing us with just enough glamorous information but never revealing too much. As each credit line appears, drifts of cigarette smoke waft across the screen, simultaneously forming, blurring and changing the text, anticipating the distorted morality and obscure intentions of the protagonists in the narrative that follows. Towards the end of the sequence, male and female hands appear, placing the cigarettes in an ashtray as they, along with the credits, continue to smoulder across the frame. The film's opening recalls the way cigarette smoke instantly conjures a specific era in which everyone was seemingly nicotine addicted, working in the present day as an instant signifier of the 1940s and 1950s, while operating on a physical level as a manifestation of the emotive impact of both smoke and monochrome cinematography itself, collecting, refracting and distorting light, beautifying the image, concealing absolute revelation and emphasising cinema's luminous artistry.

While cigarette smoke subtly blurs the image, establishing era and concealing aspects of identity and understanding in languid silver puffs, mist and fog are enabled with a denser, more ominous, dark capacity. In *The Fog* (John Carpenter, 1980) a coastal town is terrorised by shadowy creatures that emerge from a mysterious illuminated fog bank as it rolls in from the sea between the hours of midnight and 1 a.m. Light itself indicates the fog's strange nature. The first time fishermen see it swirling out at sea through the portal of their small trawler, its unusual nature is immediately visible in both its sudden appearance and in the bright lights that emanate from its centre. Although the fog impedes vision in a similar way to darkness, it does so with uncharacteristically bright illumination. The fog quickly infiltrates every corner of the boat, seeping under doorways and filtering into the engine room, extinguishing all the electric lights on the ship. Outside on deck, anonymous hook-wielding shadows emerge gradually from the mist, slaughtering two crewmen before tracking down a third man inside. Surrounded by darkness, the sailor's frightened face is intermittently illuminated by ripples of moonlight, before a monstrous shadow repeatedly stabs his vulnerable neck and the fog engulfs the ship. In this sequence one kind of opacity is replaced by another. The partial view afforded by the fog that makes boundaries indistinct, masking the identity of the killers, works in tandem with the obscurity offered by total darkness, encouraging fear through loss of sight. It is the moment just before the murder, however, not the killing itself, that is most frightening, since, without a referent, in darkness or fog, the nebulous horrors that our own minds can conjure are far more terrifying than any beings director John Carpenter can create.

As much as they suggest mystery and danger, the indistinct qualities of mist and fog often mean that they are also used in films to connote the past, in flashbacks, dreams and representations of memory. During the opening of *Rebecca* (Alfred Hitchcock, 1940) for example, when the second Mrs DeWinter's (Joan Fontaine) wistful voice-over winds its way back through time, down the curving driveway of Manderley, mist blurs the spaces between the trees on the road, seeping in grey clouds through their leaves, drawing the viewer inside her dream of the past. The diffused light clouds perception making vision unreliable, connoting the partiality of remembrance and the instability of imagination. In these evocative light conditions, outlines become vague and uncertain, people merge with their surroundings and there is a notable shift in tone from clarity to opacity: from the facts of the present to the fiction of the past.

Protagonists who disappear and reappear in mist and fog are often lost, hunted or searching. In *Insomnia* (Christopher Nolan, 2002), Detective Dormer (Al Pacino) is all three. When Dormer and his partner set a trap for Walter Finch (Robin Williams) in a fishing cabin on a deserted beach towards the start of the film, white mist descends and obscures the chase. The naturalistic light is diffused by the fog, turning the world blue-grey and working in the place of shadow to the killer's advantage as a way to hide. As Dormer and his team move in on the suspect, tripping over rocks, walking inadvertently through streams and straining to see through the mist, like the black titles that emerge out of whiteness at the start of the film, a figure slowly comes into view with his gun raised and shoots a young policeman. Dormer gives chase, squinting to see, as one would in intense sunlight or total darkness, until

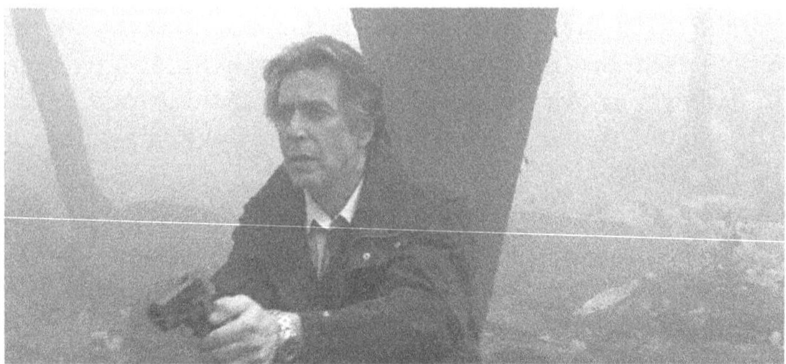

19   *Insomnia*. Detective Dormer (Al Pacino) hunts a killer in the fog

again, looming out of the fog, a figure moves. Dormer shoots and the figure falls, but, as he gets closer, he realises that he has mistakenly shot and killed his partner Eckhart. In a split second Dormer decides to cover up the accident, using the fog to conceal his crime, just like the killer. In so doing, he begins a tortuous descent into guilt-ridden sleep-deprivation and mental instability. In the mist Dormer is both hunter and hunted, predator and prey. He is struggling for information in the fog, as are we before the screen, desperate to see yet not be seen, while perception constantly shifts and falters.

The unforgiving harshness of *Insomnia*'s treacherous fogged exteriors gives way to softer, more hesitant, delicate blankets of misty childlike uncertainty in *Landscape in the Mist* (*Topio stin omichli*, Theodoros Angelopoulos, 1988). Two children run away to Germany in search of the father they have never met. Their emotional journey is marked by shifting light conditions, weather patterns and most of all by the intangible mist of the film's title. Since they have no money, Voula (Tania Palaiologou) and her little brother Alexandre (Mikhalis Zeke) are constantly ejected from the train they must catch, and so they travel by road and on foot receiving both help and abuse from the strangers they meet on their journey. Towards the end of the film, however, a young soldier gives Voula the money for the train and the children sink happily into their seats, until an announcement is made explaining that all passports – passports that Voula and Alexandre do not possess – will be checked at the border. Scrambling off the train once more, the siblings sneak past the searchlights on the border at night and clamber aboard a rowing boat. As they drift into the distance, the screen falls into total darkness before a guard spots them and a gun is fired. Desperately staring into the black space into which they sailed, we have no idea if the children have escaped or been killed. The film cuts to swirling grey mist at dawn, transforming the screen into an incomprehensible rectangle of dense shifting light, a grey area that epitomises our oscillating feelings of hope and despair. The image imitates the blank grey filmstrip that the children's friend and travelling companion Oreste gave to Alexandre earlier in the film, reflexively recalling its shape and colour as well as its representative nature as the hole their absent father has left in their lives. Slowly, almost imperceptibly, little Alexandre moves towards the screen, at first appearing then disappearing back into the mist, eventually growing more recognisable, more definite, telling his sister they have arrived in Germany and that she shouldn't be afraid, retelling 'their story', a story Voula has told him continually during their journey: 'In the beginning there was chaos. And then the light was made.' Here, the mist itself makes the light. Alexandre raises his hand and seems to touch the screen, before Voula moves forward to join him and a reverse shot reveals that Alexandre was in fact waving at a statuesque tree emerging out of the mist. As the fog lifts at the end of the film, the children run towards the tree and embrace it. Looming out of the distance like a 'latent' photographic image revealed by liquid developer, dominating the skyline, the tree operates as a stand-in for the father they searched for but never found. As the mist swirls and dissipates, the shifting grey light embodies the uncertainty of the children's fate and the intangibility of life itself.

Hidden

While unusual weather conditions like mist and fog refract and diffuse illumination, condensing it into mysterious dark swirls of opaque screen space that invoke fear, suspense and interstitial psychic states, the architecture of cinematic darkness – the location, form and shape of the environments in which protagonists hide – offers far darker situations for the cinema to explore. At key moments across the history of cinema, characters have disappeared inside wardrobes, tunnels and caves, either cowering in fear or lying in wait, trapped by the dark reflections of their thoughts as much as by the situations that have led to their entrapment. These distinctly cinematic spaces limit light and obscure vision, exuding suspense from within the darkness of their thrilling interiors.

When Laurie Strode (Jamie-Lee Curtis) scrambles behind the folding doors of a wardrobe in *Halloween* (John Carpenter, 1978) attempting to escape the masked murderer Michael (Tony Moran), in darkness she desperately ties the door handles together, shaking and panting in fear. In a reversal of the shadow bars of noir private investigator offices, pale-blue moonlight filters through the horizontal slats in the wardrobe doors, illuminating sparse areas of space, highlighting coat-hangers and dresses in the gloom. As Michael approaches, his shadow blocks yet more light and Laurie retreats further into the wardrobe shrinking into its dark recess in an attempt to hide. In this brief sequence darkness is figured as both dangerous and protective. While Michael's shadow terrifies Laurie, marking the approach of her attacker, the black depths of the wardrobe continue to offer solace and the illusion of security. Using his knife and hands Michael soon breaks in, flailing around the wardrobe's interior, until he accidentally tugs on the light switch and the safety of Laurie's hiding place is disrupted. Although this intrusive burst of light helps Laurie to see, it also highlights her vulnerability, starkly illuminating the terrifying nature of her predicament, hysterically swinging from side to side, throwing shifting shadows that further disorientate the space. As Michael clutches at Laurie, he turns the light off again, plunging them back into darkness, affording her a moment to counter-attack. As much as this is a battle to live, it is also a battle with illumination. The scene marks the way some films, especially those within the horror genre, use the architecture of darkness in domestic spaces to expressive effect. Light is directed or extinguished across interiors to create scenes that play with what we can or can't see, teasing suspense and tension from claustrophobic situations dominated by contrast and shadow.

In *Blue Velvet* (David Lynch, 1986), as much as the wardrobe in Dorothy Valens' (Isabella Rossellini's) flat offers a place for Jeffrey Beaumont (Kyle MacLachlan) to hide, it also affords him a perfect position from which to spy. On his way to break into the apartment, hoping that he might find information about a recent murder, darkness exponentially encroaches, as though he is travelling into the midnight recesses of a tunnel. The lift in Dorothy's block is out of order, so Jeffrey must climb the murky, partially lit stairs on the fire escape. Once inside her corridor the light wanes further. Passing isolated lamps that are barely glowing, apparently suffocating in the inky night that surrounds them, Jeffrey walks towards Dorothy's door, his white face shining intermittently out of the gloom like an extra beacon of illumination. Enveloped in deep-blue light, no one answers Jeffrey's knock on door 710, so he unlocks it using keys he has previously stolen. Inside, the lighting is almost non-existent, as soft and potentially suffocating as the blue velvet of the film's title. The luminous colour is dense and luxurious, oppressive in its condension of space, suggestively languid, deceptive and hallucinogenic. In almost total darkness, unable to hear Sandy Williams's (Laura Dern) car horn that should have warned him of approaching danger, Jeffrey is startled when Dorothy comes home early, and rushes inside the apparent safety of her wardrobe so he isn't seen. Once again, the horizontal slats of dark doors afford partial illumination. Thin strips of blue light seep between the gaps, casting slivers of illumination onto Jeffrey's face, recalling those that reveal and obscure Laurie's horror in *Halloween*, as he simultaneously hides and spies on the subversive sexual acts that unfold on the other side of the door. Watching Frank Booth (Edward Hopper) sucking on stimulants and abusing Dorothy in a complex display of violent mutual sexual gratification, from inside the black hole of the wardrobe, Jeffrey is in a comparable position to those on the other side, simultaneously experiencing the fear of entrapment and the sexual power of illicit vision. Both trapped and hiding, his concealed point of view makes him both the slave and master of the look. The deep-blue light amplifies the thrilling horror, recalling eerie nightmare environments, illicit negotiations inside club interiors and 'blue' movies. As the scene unfolds, on both sides of the door, the dark psychology of imprisonment combines with the voyeuristic sexual thrill of the peeping tom. Jeffrey's darkening ascent to the wardrobe in Dorothy's top-floor apartment is a metaphor for his psychic descent into the otherwise hidden depths of his own sexual deviance. Midnight-blue cinematic space amplifies the dark secrets of his unconscious. As Jeffrey explains to Sandy, 'I'm seeing something that was always hidden. I'm involved in a mystery.'

Similarly, in *The Third Man*, Harry Lime's concealed escape route becomes a chiaroscuro prison. His twisted intelligence leads to a convoluted chase. Underground, the sewers beneath Vienna offer a comparable metaphoric space of warped psychology and undisclosed secrets. With its dark passageways, dead ends and confusing configurations of tunnels and exits, the formation of the hidden sewer itself as an uninhabited and mysterious replica city of shadows, emphasises the film's narrative of lies and double-crossings, reflecting complex character motivations. Although the space above ground harbours more secrets than the area below, the construction of the tunnels exacerbates suspense by emphasising a plethora of atmospheric and expressive stark chiaroscuro illumination. Shadows, silhouettes, black holes of screen space, foggy puffs of smoke, streams of watery illumination, wet shiny walls, sweeping cones of torchlight: in the space of the sewer each technique of contrast is employed for maximum visual impact. As Harry skids away from the light down blind alleys, shadows on the seeping walls duplicate the number of guards, while curved ceilings magnify their shouts so that they look and sound like an army advancing. Light reflects off splashed water as Harry runs, spraying white illumination into the black air around him. Briefly pausing in a cavernous space, Harry is suddenly unsure which way to turn. Confronted on all sides by black tunnels of different sizes and shapes, their yawning mouths echoing with the sound of the guard's unrelenting search, Harry accidentally chooses the one in which his old friend Holly Martins is waiting. At the end of the sequence, Harry is shot in iconic silhouette as he runs towards the light for the first time. His graphic black form falls to the ground, until he musters the strength to go on, dragging himself up a metal staircase. As his fingers hopelessly grope the fresh air outside the tunnels, the contrasting bars of illumination and shadow that bounce off the iron grill above criss-cross Harry's face sealing his fate.

The cinematic architecture of the divided character of darkness as an impenetrable yet protective prison is explored to great lengths in Christopher Nolan's *Batman Begins* (2005). Batman's iconology – his mask, cape, car and cave – envelope the superhero in darkness, offering him security and strength through anonymity, while at the same time isolating him in pitch-black spaces within which his split psyche struggles to cope. When Bruce Wayne (Christian Bale) falls down a well as a young boy at the start of the film, a dark cave gapes from a hole in the wall, scaring him with its unknowable blackness from which a thousand webbed wings ominously whisper. As Bruce's fear escalates, the camera zooms closer, apparently struggling to see into the dark void ahead. Suddenly the winged sounds take shape when a flock of bats burst out of the cave in a flurry of darkness, swamping the screen and dimming the bright sky above, until Bruce wakes from this familiar nightmare as an older man.

Throughout the film, multiple connections and references are made between darkness and mystery or fear. Bruce Wayne's saviour and trainer, Ra's Al Ghul, heads 'The League of Shadows', a company of men dedicated to instilling fear in those who deserve it using dark methods of deception, invisibility and force. On separate occasions, during conversations with Bruce, both Ra's Al Ghul and crime boss Carmine Falconi connect fear to a lack of understanding and a loss of sight. Ra's states: 'Men fear most what they cannot see', while Falconi notes, 'You always fear what you don't understand', reiterating John Alton's comments that link cinematic darkness with suspense and a fear of the unknown. It is in an attempt to conquer his fears that Bruce embraces his alter ego Batman, returning to the spot at the bottom of the well where his nightmares first began. Staring into the black heart of the cave once more, Bruce summons the courage to crawl into the darkness, an act that is tantamount to walking into the dark spaces of his own psyche, towards his past as a little boy who was once afraid. In the dank cave, deep underground, Bruce's presence scares the bats and once again they surge around him in a swarm of blackened beating wings. His resolute stance of acceptance, arms outstretched, head thrown back, eyes closed, surrounded by shifting shadows, marks the moment he conquers his fear of the unknown and the beginning of his transformation into Batman. Frightening Detective Gordon and criminals alike with his ability to disappear into and emerge from areas of pitch-black space, swirling his cape to create swathes of enveloping shadow that blot out the sky, standing masked and alone atop towering skyscrapers at midnight: in the guise of Batman, Bruce becomes (as Ra's Al Ghul suggests he must at the start of the film) 'one with the darkness'.

Pitch-black

Much of the dramatic tension in *Batman Begins* emerges from Bruce Wayne's determination to hide in the darkness as Batman: his wish to remain anonymous, and our own persistent desire (one that mirrors those of his opponents and associates alike) to unmask him, to see through his dark disguise, to revel in the revelation of the man behind the myth. The withholding of information only intensifies our need to seek answers. In the cinema, a total lack of illumination removes familiar references, encouraging our imaginations to fill in the gap, as we anticipate the return of visual information, a moment of relief when the screen will once more be filled with light. Darkness encourages a sensual guessing game. A key technique of the horror genre is the use of areas of dark screen space as sites of intrigue and anxiety from which we suspect a monster or murderer might attack. In *The Fog*, as Kathy Williams (Janet Leigh) searches the church for Father Malone, she stands by pews on the left-hand side of the frame, calling out his name, while a large area of darkness dominates the space to the right. When Father Malone suddenly emerges from the void, he makes both Kathy and the audience jump. Time and again in the horror film, dark voids are employed in this way, as tools of suspense and shock, playing with our conviction that an absence of illumination goes hand in hand with imminent danger.

Starved of a key sense, without sight our hearing is elevated. As we struggle to see and are denied illumination, our ears take over and we rely on sound to construct a picture of the action unfolding on-screen. In *The Blair Witch Project*, darkness itself is the enemy, since no monster or aggressor is ever pictured on-screen. On the third perilous night the three student filmmakers spend lost in the woods, they hear the ominous noise of wood snapping outside their tent and leave its relative safety to investigate. Using two low-budget digital video cameras – one colour and one black and white – to film their experiences, they creep into the darkness of the woods. A single top-mounted light attached to one of the cameras is the only source of illumination, bouncing off pale skin and white branches as Heather (Heather Donohue) walks towards the sounds, moving forward, shouting 'Hello' into the terrifying pitch-black spaces between trees. In the absence of a visible threat, danger is embodied in sounds, so that the rustling noise of branches and twigs cracking, or animals and people crying out, provide a picture of the potential horrors unfolding outside the tent. Darkness works in tandem with technology to distort vision. The pixelated grain and pitching hand-held sway of the low-budget cameras decrease visibility so that even total darkness seems to move and shift on the screen, evoking cinema's ontological instability as a ghostly medium capable of resurrecting the dead. When Josh (Joshua Leonard) goes missing his absence is more frightening than the visual experience of his death or the discovery of a body; the imagined sight of violence becomes more terrifying than violence itself, as Heather sobs into the camera, 'I'm too scared to close my eyes and I'm scared to open them.' At the end of the film when Heather and Mike (Michael Williams) go in search of Josh in an abandoned house, its yawning glass-less windows form pitch-black squares of darkness within which our deepest fears manifest. The lack of visual information is terrifying. As Heather runs down to the basement after Mike, desperate to save Josh, the sound of screaming intensifies, while her own fear causes increasing camera-shake, off-kilter framing and rapid movements that further distort our vision. At the bottom of the stairs Mike is just visible standing in the corner with his back to us, before there is a devastating thud and Heather's camera hits the ground in a confused composition of black and grey shapes, marking the end of the whirring tape and the end of her life, fulfilling the legend that the Blair Witch made children face the darkness of a wall before murdering their friends.

In the cinema and in life, when staring into total darkness we yearn for the void to be filled; for illumination to offer vision and knowledge, for light to mark our way and keep us safe.

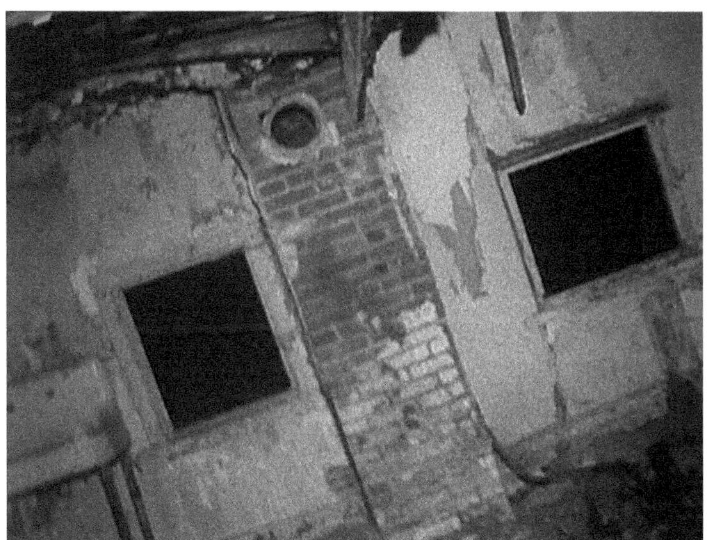

20   *The Blair Witch Project*. Pitch-black voids manifest our deepest fears

When shadows stretch across the screen, when fog blurs vision, when architecture conceals, when black holes gape, in anxiety, fear and confusion we struggle to make sense of the vanishing images on the screen. The shades that hint at presence also evoke the unknowable nothingness of death. And yet, these modes of darkness are not terrifying in themselves, they merely offer a platform upon which the dreams and nightmares of our own imagination can perform. Most night terrors are ones of our own making. During the blue-black moments of *Blue Velvet* or *The Fog* or *The Blair Witch Project*, or while watching the orchestral pitch-black opening minutes of *2001: A Space Odyssey*, just before the sun rises in space, our eyes strain into the abyss, struggling to see, longing for illumination to solidify presence, to provoke recognition, to confirm and construct the images, sights and emotions that we have come to the cinema to imagine and experience.

Notes

1 Alton, *Painting with Light*, pp. 44–5.
2 D. Frampton, *Filmosophy* (London: Wallflower, 2006), p. 119.
3 Sternberg, 'More Light', 70.
4 Keating, *Hollywood Lighting*, pp. 75 and 77.
5 See J. Root, 'Film Noir', in Cook (ed), *Cinema Book*, p. 305.
6 See M. Bould, *Film Noir: From Berlin to Sin City* (London and New York: Wallflower, 2005), p. 60.
7 As Mike O'Pray has noted, 'It should be remarked that film noir's lighting style is not as defining as was once thought. It was used long before the period in question by many other kinds of film. What was the case, however, was that such a chiaroscuro lighting was combined with a certain theme or subject-matter. The style has a film history status which should be treated cautiously as more historical work has uncovered the distorted view of the context in which such films were made' (*Film, Form and Phantasy*, p. 202).
8 Patrick Keating divides the history of film noir criticism into two areas: the 'expressionist' account, including essays written by Janey Place, Lowell Peterson and Paul Schrader and the 'revisionist' account, including writing by Barry Salt, Marc Vernet and Thomas Elsaesser (*Hollywood Lighting*, pp. 244–5).
9 See E. A. Wallis Budge, *The Egyptian Book of the Dead (The Papyrus of Ani)* (New York: Dover, 1969), pp. lvi and lxvii.
10 See C. W. Eliot (ed), *Homer (Harvard Classics)* (Danbury, CT: Grolier, 1980), pp. 156–7.
11 V. I. Stoichita, *A Short History of the Shadow* (London: Reaktion, 1997), p. 131.
12 O. Rank, *The Double: A Psychoanalytic Study* (North Carolina: University of North Carolina Press, 1971), pp. 50 and 58.
13 *Ibid.*
14 E. Rutherford, *Silhouette* (New York: Rizzoli International Publications, 2009), p. 8.

5 The past

<blockquote>

He remembers those vanished years. As though looking through a dusty window-pane, the past is something he could see but not touch. And everything he sees is blurred and indistinct.

(closing title, *In the Mood for Love* (Wong Kar-wai, 2000)

</blockquote>

<blockquote>

the past is forever a diffused memory, a happening that is thought uncertainly as any act of remembering is – but distinctly a film memory … a plastic past remembered through cine-images.

(Daniel Frampton, 'Colour', *New Scholarship from BFI Research*, 1995)

</blockquote>

Films set in the past often indicate their nostalgic tense with a light-associated absence: a lack of colour, a loss of visual definition, a subdued tonal palette, a literal dearth of illumination. While total cinematic darkness offers mystery and suspense via visual negation and imaginative transposition, a limited loss of light represents our incapacity to fully record, represent or recreate the past. Darkness provides an absolute space, a gap that imagination and supposition must fill, whereas barely there illumination marks a move from such absolute visual freedom to subtle suggestion. Here light stakes its claim as a key element of cinema aesthetics, using visual quality to directly reflect the way we understand and interact with the past. Shifts and losses in the quality, texture and strength of cinematic light denote accordant temporal shifts in the representation of history. The instability and uncertainty of remembrance is visualised, just as with mist and fog, via monochrome cinematography, in a blown-out haze of light, or in slightly lit scenes that associate darkly coloured illumination with repressed emotion and sudden bouts of longing. In this context partial light connotes the partiality of memory. Insubstantial illumination (or diffused, indefinite textures resulting from the oppositional qualities of extreme saturated light) ensures that these images and the characters and environments within them, just like the past they seek to represent, remain almost out of sight, situated between presence and invisibility. In the films discussed below, cinematic expression mirrors the mind as it struggles to retrieve indistinct experiences and feelings, as it gropes in the gloom for luminous images that might reaffirm present identity through a confirmation of the existence of the past.

Stripped entirely of colour, vanishing in pastel shades or clinging to the Technicolor hues of the past, these films are themselves nostalgic for a disappearing analogue era, an era filled with darkrooms and ammonium thiosulfate, a time of fixer, developer and chemical processing, an almost past when black-and-white photographs were regularly printed from negatives onto paper in order to be held in the palm of a hand or cherished in a frame. While natural and artificial lighting on location or on set has always contributed to the texture, atmosphere and emotion of the film image, its original ontology as a medium defined by celluloid, filters, exposure times, emulsion and light-sensitive chemicals has also affected the way we experience illumination in the cinema. Fast or slow film stock results in a high- or low-contrast image, while the density of greys and the intensity of colours on the screen are directly affected by both the amount of exposure time the film receives during shooting and the length of time the print is developed. Similarly, the use of both opaque and colour gelatine filters blocks or intensifies certain colour waves from the negative, transforming the shades and hues that we see, washing artificially coloured light across the screen. Over time, changes in processing technology and the creation of new film stocks and filter techniques as well as recent digital post-production methods have meant that films from the 1940s and 1950s look different to those of the 1970s or the 1990s, not just because of shifting acting styles, set designs, countries of origin or directorial style, but also as a result of the way light itself has been refracted through evolving light-sensitive film material.

Two modes of image nostalgia are thus at work in the memory film. On the one hand, in monochrome or substantially faded colour films like *Raging Bull* (Martin Scorsese, 1980) or *Saving Private Ryan* (Steven Spielberg, 1998) that aim to represent the past as it has been recorded in images, as well as cinema's own monochrome past, the black-and-white or sepia photograph becomes a touchstone for familiar, apparently authentic historical re-enactment. On the other, in artificially lit, darkly coloured films set in the past like *Far from Heaven* (Todd Haynes, 2002) or *In the Mood for Love* (*Fa yeung nin wa*, Wong Kar-wai, 2000), filmic history itself is revisited in order to authenticate images in the present. In the former, cinema is nostalgic for the simplistic graphic forms of a medium that has become associated with both gritty photojournalistic realism and the creative artifice of art photography, while in the latter cinema embraces its own illuminated technical past of evolving celluloid as a reference point for the contemporary representation of different eras. In both instances the past is defined not by the light and colour of the actual past, but by the past as it has been recorded and reconfigured in photographs and on the screen: a constructed, prosthetic, photo-cinematic image past.

In a reversal of the previous chapter which grew darker as it advanced, moving from the light and shade of the shadow to pitch-black voids of cinematic space, this chapter evolves towards illumination, gaining light from a position of darkness as the discussion progresses. As much as cinema represents the past with light-associated absences, it also marks the passage of time with a lack of light and a return to black space. Temporality itself – either the motion of time on-screen or the visualisation of times-gone-by – is figured by a gap or a loss of vision. As such, this chapter starts with the total darkness of the elliptical fade and gets brighter, or at least more defined, as it moves through sections on contemporary monochrome films and muted representations of the past before concluding with a discussion of intensely coloured emotive memory films and moments of darkness within them. The transition from darkness to luminous colour begins with a fade to black; an ellipsis that marks a momentary yet absolute loss of light, an absence that signifies temporal progression, a black gap without representation across which time flows.

Ellipsis: back to black

Cinema operates within two modes of temporality: the time of watching (the spectatorial view), and the time within the image (the filmic view).[1] In the former, the spectator is the pivot around which temporality revolves, time is understood through their subjective experience of watching a film on-screen, it unravels in line with the rest of recorded human experience; an hour is an hour, a minute is a minute, a second is a second. In the latter, the film dictates temporality, time unravels within the narrative on-screen, it expands and contracts, bending to the whim of the filmmaker; an hour can be a lifetime, a minute can be a week, a second can be a day. As cinematic language evolved, certain visual techniques began to denote particular temporal shifts. In order to compress time, filmmakers devised breaks in the narrative flow, gaps in time and space within which days, weeks, months and locations might pass or change in seconds. One of the key aspects of film language initially employed by Hollywood's influential continuity system and subsequently found in almost all modes and genres was a momentary fade to black, an ellipsis used to mark a fissure in the passage of on-screen time. During an ellipsis for a brief moment the scene on-screen disappears along with the light. It is as though the film itself is blinking, as though a heavy lid momentarily closes over the camera's lens, shutting out the light. When the image returns from darkness, characters and objects have either slightly shifted or the scene has changed entirely. Illumination retreats and is instead briefly replaced by a black void within which the present accelerates away from the past towards the future. The dark screen becomes a temporal bridge.

In *Bicycle Thieves*, after Ricci and his wife Maria retrieve his much-needed bicycle from the pawnbrokers at the start of the film they go to the fortune teller so that Maria can pay for her accurate prediction that Ricci would get a job. Afterwards, on the street outside, Maria gets on the front of Ricci's bicycle and they cycle together towards the camera, smiling in harmony at the prospect of a regular income. Just before they ride out of shot, as they emerge from the darkness of cobbled side streets into the open sunshine of the foreground, the screen fades to black and everything is momentarily hidden from view. In total darkness a few seconds of spectatorial time elapse before the image fades up on Ricci's son Bruno preparing his dad's bicycle for work. 'It's 6.30, Bruno', Ricci whispers, emphasising his rush to work as well as the sudden temporal and spatial shift from a sunny afternoon street to a gloomy bedroom at dawn that the ellipsis made possible. On-screen an entire night has passed during an instant of darkness. The absent light of a fade to black replaces the inactivity of a night when nothing happens. A stream of light-blackened photograms flows through the projector. In this flash of darkness we imagine the Riccis restless in their sheet-less beds, the anxiety, excitement and hope of a new job and new prospects perhaps preventing a good night's sleep. During the course of the film a similar black space marks the end of each on-screen day and the beginning of the next, sewing together days with absent nights, connecting otherwise disjointed periods of time and space, propelling the Riccis towards future despair, closing the gap between yesterday, today and tomorrow.

In the post-jumpcut era, after Eisenstein and *Breathless* and *Point Blank* (John Boorman, 1967), the ellipsis still endures across continents and genres as a key technique of temporal cinematic shorthand; a brief return to darkness through which cinema speaks a common language of compressed time and space. At the same time, however, the ellipsis has itself been subject to deviation and experimentation. The pause in pace and temporal shift that its loss of light suggests offers other avenues for visual communication. In Chapter 3 it was noted that Kieslowśki's *Three Colours: Blue* (1993) follows Julie's luminous symphonic memories with a sudden fade to black in which the force of her emotions erases the lit image from the screen. As much as these ellipses mark a potentially unrepresentable surge in feeling, they also mark abrupt changes in Julie's psyche, fissures between her past and present self; shifts not in time, but in emotional tempo. Four key moments of interaction are marked in the film with a fade to black. The first occurs between a simple greeting of *bonjour* and Julie's subdued reply. Convalescing on her blue balcony, consumed by the remembered light and sound of her husband's symphony, Julie is startled by the arrival of a journalist who wants to write an article about her husband's final work. The woman's 'hello' tears Julie out of reverie, eradicating expressive lighting, pushing her back to harsh reality, while the music thunders on across a lengthy black screen. Torn away from a moment of affecting personal memory, the difference in Julie's expression before and after the ellipsis is arresting; then she was stunned and vacant, now she is cold and indifferent. As the journalist says to Julie, 'You've changed.' Unlike the traditional ellipses of *Bicycle Thieves,* time and place do not shift across this black space. Instead, the darkness marks a sudden yet fundamental emotional transition from the shocked devastation of private loss to the cold apathy of public grief.

As Julie's journey from stricken widow to functioning individual progresses, Kieslowśki's fades to black become connotative of positive mental developments as opposed to negative experience. Whereas the black space at first reinforced Julie's isolation and detachment, it now begins to emphasise her recovery. Where once she was closed down and unresponsive, now, slowly, she begins to open up. She meets Antoine (Yann Tregouet) in a café who presents her with a treasured necklace she lost during the car crash. He was there when her husband died and asks if there is anything she'd like to ask him. 'No', she bluntly replies, just before the image disappears into a concerto-filled fade. When the screen reappears, Julie apologises and decides to give Antoine the necklace to keep. This act of kindness and transition is followed by two more fades. During the first, Sandrine (Florence Pernel) finds Julie in the pool. She asks 'Have you been crying?', before the black screen and the music return. Afterwards Julie leans on her and sobs, finally accepting some help. Before the fourth and final black screen, Olivier (Benoît Régent), Julie's lover, asks her what she wants to do about her husband's mistress. Her face leans away from the camera, her expression concealed as the light leaves and the concerto crescendos. During the moment of darkness she makes up her mind. Her face swivels towards us. 'Meet her', she resolutely replies. Each ellipsis offers Julie a moment of respite and quiet contemplation, a moment to gather her thoughts, a moment that demonstrates her shifting state of mind. Although time and place remain the same, after each fade to black Julie is different. The fades chart the partial recoveries and devastating relapses of grief: the way abject sorrow at the loss of a loved one can come upon us, unbidden, as all memories can, shocking experience in jolts of dark emotion, while transforming our sense of self. Darkness offers redemption and release. When the light returns, tears fall, Julie's head turns towards us, a smile appears, a decision is made – the black screen designates change and progress, it marks a before and after, a past and a present.

Monochrome

Light is colour. As Roger Bacon, Isaac Newton and Johann Wolfgang von Goethe variously attested via observations of water and prisms, when rays of light are split apart, its construction is revealed in fractured wavelengths of violet, blue, cyan, green, yellow, orange and red.[2] When the coloured parts of the spectrum are removed in monochrome photographic forms, the light that remains is only a partial representation; something is missing or hidden, and this absence pulls realism apart at the seams. In black and white everything on the screen is defined by the relationship between light and shade. Although the coloured spectrum is suppressed, the dialectic of a limited palette only emphasises further the power and significance of illumination. The world is condensed into the mythic simplicity of darkness and light, in shades of white, grey and black, heightening the impact of expressive light on the atmospheres, emotions and narratives displayed. Accordingly, monochrome discussions are dominated by issues of historical veracity and cultural nostalgia. Most recent black-and-white cinema longs for both the apparent straightforwardness of the past and its artistic monochrome artifice, illuminating the relationship between cinematic and photographic modes, while encouraging debate about the construction of memory via mediums of light in the post-digital age.

At the heart of discussions regarding the death of film and photography in the period leading up to cinema's centenary in the early 1990s – the 'loss of the real' in the digital age – lay an inherent nostalgia for the optical and ontological qualities of the analogue, black-and-white photograph. Along with anxieties regarding the replacement of negatives and prints by intangible, ethereal data, there was a longing not for the past, but for a past mode of representation.[3] Contemporary commentators seemed to be mourning not the loss of actual photographic realism (which had never truly existed), but rather the emotional loss of a kind of imagined, fetishised photographic truth and aura, elevated by theorists such as Susan Sontag and Roland Barthes, the most visible element of which is a monochrome palette.[4] Pam Cook has defined nostalgia as 'a state of longing for something that is known to be irretrievable, but is sought anyway'.[5] In this context, however, the factual and realistic photographic truth of the monochrome past that seemed to be longed for never actually existed. The black-and-white image has always been a constructed version of reality. It envisions a past that has been stripped of colour, a past that is reimagined in form and line, contrast and opposition, light and shade.

Due to the mechanical ontology of cinema and photography, the content, form and style of the images that are preserved shift apace with contemporary fashion and technological development. As a result, as photographic technology develops, so too does the way society remembers the past. In this environment, technical limitations become cultural connotations. The technological break that occurred in visual culture when colour was introduced on a large scale, along with an enduring monochrome preference in 'serious' photojournalism and art photography, resulted in the black-and-white image becoming historically connotative of a specific period of the past, while epitomising notions of truth and gravitas. In other words, all forms of cinema and photography, from photojournalism, to art cinema, to advertising and documentaries (and indeed their relative mediums, television and the internet), are part of the creation of an image-based, technologically driven collective memory through which history is filtered, of which the most overt visual signifier of the past has become the presentation of the world in black and white. The two cornerstones of the black-and-white photograph – a photojournalistic drive to record and report on the one hand, and a desire to distinguish the medium both as art and as distinct from painting, on the other – have created a photographically remembered past that emphasises a monochrome representation of history. It is this past that monochrome films of the last forty years seek to retrieve, replicate and renew.

The monochrome films discussed below were inspired by both a photojournalistic documentary aesthetic and the prevalence of black-and-white media images (on television, and in advertisements) from the past, while they are simultaneously influenced by a sense of emotional nostalgia for noirish film aesthetics and the grit and grain of low-budget 1960s cinema. What emerges is the sense that the black-and-white past, as Pam Cook and Celia Lury have argued with regard to media-based reproductions, is a prosthetic construct, a manipulated version of history built with layers of imagery that continues to be reinforced in the present by new films that seek to authenticate their narratives with a monochrome palette.[6] In order to understand how the actual past is visualised in memory we must first look at the way that it has come to be represented in contemporary fictional versions of history. What emerges is a presentation of the past that is bound up in black-and-white televisual, filmic and photographic tropes that represent history, not through actual realism, but through the remembered emotive realism of the illuminated image.

The slow-motion black-and-white title sequence of *Raging Bull* (Martin Scorsese, 1980) epitomises the layered photo-cinematic nostalgia of the monochrome image. As Jake LaMotta (Robert De Niro) bobs and weaves behind the harsh black horizontal ropes of the boxing ring, the heady strings of Pietro Mascagni's *Cavalleria Rusticana* flow over his languid movements, emphasising this dream-like atmospheric haze of remembrance. Flashbulbs occasionally burst in the smoke behind him, punctuating the muted greyness with pops of illumination that recall his tumultuous life in the

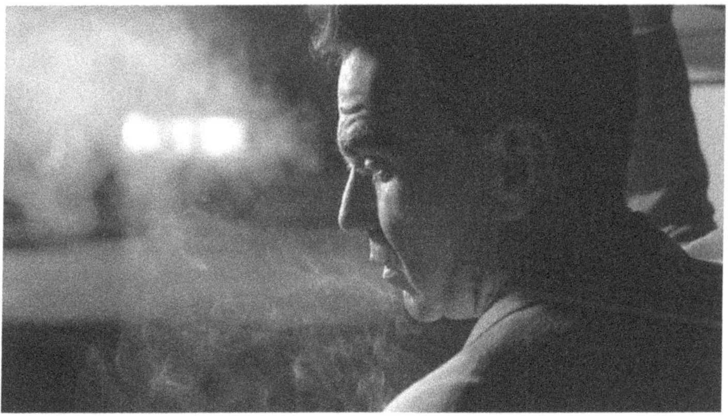

21   *The Man Who Wasn't There*. Ed Crane (Billy-Bob Thornton) thinks and smokes in nostalgic monochrome

spotlight. The lighting in these opening minutes is striking in its muted subtlety, diffusing off the hazy smoke, reflecting the wholly cinematic spectacle of his aestheticised slow-motion movements. As LaMotta bounces and struts behind bars, he is figured as at once free and trapped: both master of his fluid body, and slave to his uncontrollable emotions. The nature of the monochrome image emphasises (as does the photographic sepia freeze-frame at the end of *Butch Cassidy and the Sundance Kid* (George Roy Hill, 1969), and the photographically inspired black-and-white dialectic of *Schindler's List* (Steven Spielberg, 1993)) LaMotta's status as a real person, a historical figure who exists and is remembered in photographs and filmstrips from a bygone era, a man locked down in past times.

The Man Who Wasn't There (Joel Coen, 2001) imagines a more artificial and overtly cinematically inspired black-and-white past. The film's monochrome cinematography is used to depict not just a sense of historical verisimilitude (so that the film looks the way a contemporary audience used to seeing black-and-white images from this era might imagine it would look), but also to communicate an artistic level of craftsmanship within which composition, form and shadow are of paramount importance to the film's construction. Through its use of noirish lighting, temporal experimentation and wistful voice-over, the film attempts to recreate the stylised, artificial atmosphere of the filmic past.

Set in 1949, just after the end of the Second World War, the film depicts a few weeks in the singular life of Ed Crane (Billy Bob Thornton), a quiet yet disillusioned barber whose life disintegrates after he attempts to blackmail his wife's lover in order to raise $10,000 with which he hopes to set up a revolutionary dry-cleaning business. Crane is frequently filmed in shadow, leaning in doorways, standing on the margins, listening to other people talk, the smoke from his ever-present cigarette seemingly the only signifier of his presence. The combination of black-and-white cinematography, diaphanous cigarette smoke and reflective voice-over, works to create a dream-like version of the late 1940s that is slow and thoughtful, simplistic and fantastical. With cinematographer Roger Deakins, the Coen brothers manipulate and accentuate the image-based systems of black-and-white remembrance I have been discussing. Instead of using monochrome cinematography to authenticate their version of the past, they use it as a coded signifier of sympathetic historical pastiche: their chiaroscuro monochrome is excessively grey and lustrous, their characters (especially Ed, in a reflection of the cigarette smoke that surrounds him), move incredibly slowly and their improbable narrative of murder and redemption all work against the association of black and white with realism, instead emphasising their artistic, cinematically inspired, noirish, postmodern intentions. The film is as much concerned with the simplistic duality of black and white, as it is with the artistic potential of monochrome as a transformative signifier of contemporary nostalgia.

Since the mid 1990s when increasing numbers of post-produced converted black-and-white cinematic images emerged, some critics have argued that digital monochrome

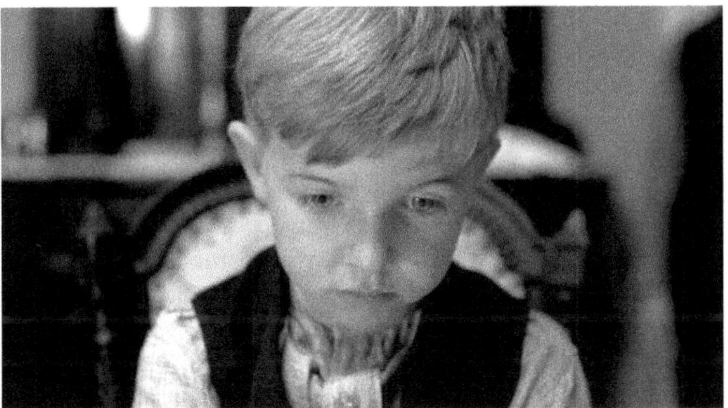

22   *The White Ribbon/Das Weiße Band*. Gustav (Thibault Sérié) waits to be punished by his father in digitally reproduced black and white

lacks the nostalgic authenticity evoked by film.[7] This computer-generated monochrome image in which film is either stripped of colour in post-production, or 'painted' with black-and-white digital effects, for some eschews both the grit and grain of photojournalistic realism and the wistful dream-like recollections of the photographically inspired reconstructed past. At the same time, however, the digital monochrome film offers something different. It presents the spectator with a new way of understanding and valuing the black-and-white image that uses both technological advances and more traditional systems of visual craftsmanship to complicate contemporary modes of seeing.

Recently, digital techniques and the talents of the technicians involved in manipulating the image have improved so that in certain circumstances it is increasingly difficult to tell if a film has either been shot on monochrome stock or transformed into black and white in post-production. Due to the insufficient sensitivity of black-and-white film stock to low light levels, Michael Haneke's *The White Ribbon* (*Das Weiße Band*, 2009) was filmed in colour and converted, a fact that is belied by the film's densely lustrous monochrome imagery that intentionally recalls the austere 1920s and 1930s portrait photography of August Sander.[8] As Haneke himself explains regarding his decision to use black-and-white imagery, 'the viewer knows the story is not "reality" but a memory, an artefact created by someone. I felt that was necessary because this was a film set in the past. It's the same thing with using black and white rather than colour – it reminds you it's not reality you're seeing but something artificial.'[9] For Haneke, digital black-and-white cinema *adds* artistic value since it highlights the ability of the monochrome image to transform coloured reality into the constructed nostalgia of form and shadow.

In Robert Rodriguez and Frank Miller's noir-inspired *Sin City* (Frank Miller and Robert Rodriguez, 2005), the on-screen relationship between monochrome imagery, nostalgia and artifice is further complicated with the addition of both comic-book inspiration and computer-generated technology that entirely divorces the black-and-white image from its connections to photojournalistic truth and instead artistically manipulates monochrome as though it were expressive, painterly colour. The film uses digital chiaroscuro black-and-white cinematography and instants of luscious, saturated, painterly colour to reimagine three of Frank Miller's iconic comics: *That Yellow Bastard* (1996), *The Hard Goodbye* (1991–92) and *The Big Fat Kill* (1994–95).

Almost everything in the film was shot on green-screen, allowing Rodriguez and Miller to use small, highly controlled sets where the actors interact intimately with each other, before transforming the material in post-production so that Miller's signature comic style of moody, graphic lighting and fantasy cityscapes could be realised with the help of state-of-the-art computer technology. A limited, predominantly monochrome environment mirrors the limited emotional existence of the characters in which polarised boundaries of good and evil are still very much enforced.[10] When colour does appear, it jumps out of the monochrome world, saturating the coloured object, body part or excretion of choice with intense, vibrant hues that look like splattered paint. Flashes of emotional colour, especially anger or intense love are rendered only sparingly, most often visualised as brooding, vampish red on women's lips that recall the blood that pumps out of the bodies of the broken, beaten anti-heroes.

However emotionally invigorating these accents of colour are, the most intense moments in the film are signalled not with colour, but with a return to a purely graphic world that is devoid of almost all detail, except the fundamental dialectic between darkness and illumination. When Dwight nearly drowns in oil in The Pitt after trying to hide the bodies of the policemen that the prostitutes of Old Town have accidentally killed, he slips under the surface and loses consciousness and the filmic world shifts from detailed monochrome and colour to stark black and white, so that he appears like a white stencilled figure floating in a sea of black tar, recalling the hard simplistic oppositions of the silhouette. In the final moments of *That Yellow Bastard* when Hartigan finally decides to end it all and shoot himself, again the film reverts to collage-like white images on a black background, as the bullet exits his head and he falls to the ground surrounded by graphic mounds of snow. In these moments computer-generated imagery (CGI) makes the visual and aesthetic quality of monochrome different. It divorces the image from its chemical referent, distancing cinema and its association to the historical black and white of the photograph from its connection with factual record and imprinting the image on-screen with the painterly, malleable qualities of art and design. Instead of referencing the mechanical, the image looks and feels handmade, so that in *Sin City*, the use of both CGI and digital techniques seem to push the image past the realm of the photo-cinematic and towards a new kind of visual spectacle that can visually reimagine graphic forms and historical literary genres as much as is it can display an image with light.

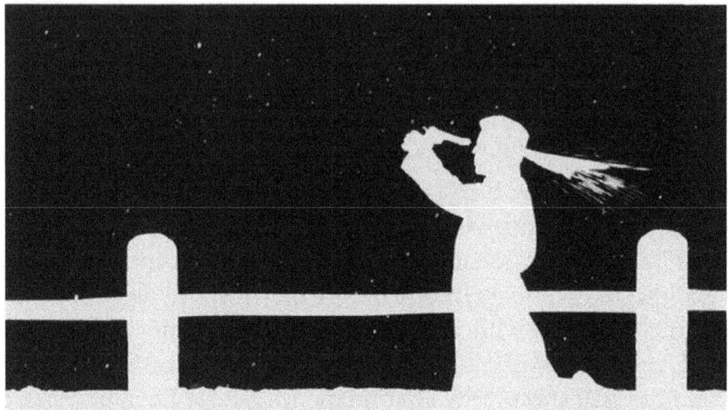

23   *Sin City.* Hartigan (Bruce Willis) puts a bullet through his head in graphic collage

The desire to document and preserve history is most evident in contemporary black-and-white films that directly recall the serious intent, yet partial capacity of black-and-white photojournalism to report the world in form and shadow, turning the monochrome photographic past into a cinematic fetish. These films continue to use black-and-white cinematography to transform personal and cultural memory through a sense of sombre historical authenticity, while simultaneously reminding us of the irrepressible impact of photography on the formation of cultural memory. As Celia Lury notes, 'The assumption here, then, is that the photograph, more than merely representing, has taught us a way of seeing (Ihde, 1995), and that this way of seeing has transformed contemporary self-understandings.'[11] The direct, oppositional qualities of the monochrome image are used to not only nostalgically recall the past, but to also address more modern concerns regarding the nature of social and cultural memory on a graphic visual level; at the same time, advances in digital technology indicate a sophisticated, more complex, somewhat plastic return to hand-crafted techniques that begin to mark the black-and-white image as a non-indexical sign. In this way digital black-and-white cinematography can be read as a shared visual language that helps to immediately situate the spectator in a recognisable time period, just as it works as a tool through which contemporary issues of authenticity, artifice and nostalgia can be explored. Ultimately, through these monochrome palettes, and their intertextual photo-filmic style of referencing and remembering history, the 'remembered realism' of illuminated images becomes the most real, most emotive and most evocative version of historical remembrance.

Muted light

For certain filmmakers, just as the past remains a photo-centric black-and-white concept, there are some subjects that can only be adequately remembered in muted colour and indistinct light. In these films lighting techniques reflect a number of uncertainties, figuring the indefinite experience of remembrance alongside an anxiety regarding the vibrant or distinct visual representation of traumatic historical events. At the same time, the past is often imagined in pared-down hues and subtle, diffused lighting in order to emphasise the assumed glamour of previous eras, tinting history in nostalgic, wistful shades. In each case, whether the film's narrative arc and aesthetic preference is horrifying or luxurious, the past seems barely there, visually out of reach, an almost untouchable realm that is forever retreating from the present.

Saving Private Ryan begins with a melancholy trumpet and an American flag. The star-spangled banner ripples in the breeze, consuming the frame as it unfurls between our eyes and the sun-filled sky. The flag diffuses illumination, subduing the strength of the sun's rays so that the reds and blues of its fabric are bleached out, so that the stars and stripes struggle for representation against a luminous background. This visual uncertainty anticipates the moral ambiguity of the Second

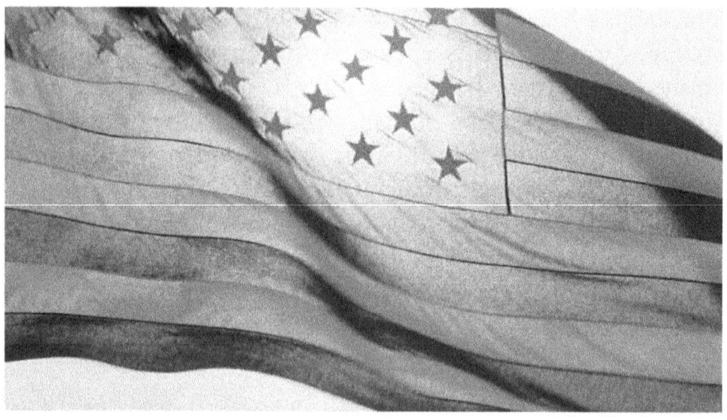

24 *Saving Private Ryan*. Diffused illumination and a bleached-out star-spangled banner question the moral certitude of war

World War experiences that follow. The all-encompassing, yet barely visible American flag is Spielberg's patriotic metaphor for faded glory, for resolute courage under fire, for the apparently indefatigable American spirit in the face of adversity and the certainty of national identity amidst the blurred moral boundaries of war.

On Omaha beach the muted colour palette and indistinct blown-out illumination continues. The browns, greens and blues of director of photography Janusz Kaminski's filters merge with the diffused colours of the dirty sand, officers' uniforms and waves that are slowly turning red-brown from all the blood in the water. Like the men on the beach, the light in this opening scene is cold, drained of energy and stunned in a reflection of Robert Capa's shaky D-day landing photographs that were damaged during processing and that partly inspired the divorced brutality of this opening scene. Even the blood spurting from open wounds and blown-off limbs is dull and lacking in vibrancy, quickly dispersing into the sea and the sand, its on-screen power filtering across the screen as it merges and dissipates into everything it touches. In the predominantly monochrome film *Schindler's List,* Spielberg felt that the horror of the Holocaust could not be represented in colour: 'The Holocaust … was life without light. For me the symbol of life is color. That's why a film about the Holocaust has to be in black-and-white.'[12] Similarly, in *Saving Private Ryan* it seems that although colour is present, it is suppressed and diluted, *almost* monochrome, as though Spielberg is unable to imagine war in anything but photographically inspired degrees of black and white that seem to work as visual markers for his own reverential feelings towards the subject matter. In Spielberg's films the absence or intensity of cinematic light and colour is directly attached to the emotions he has towards the narratives he depicts. Abject horror and apparently clear-cut represen-tations of good and evil are depicted accordingly in oppositional shades of black and white, while the rather muddier moral waters of warfare itself are presented in pale colours and washed-out illumination. In each case there is a sense that our absence and distance from historical events necessitates partial representation. Full colour and bright illumination is somehow disrespectful. In order to honour those that were there, we can only represent and remember the past in pieces. Since our knowledge of these events (apart from eyewitness accounts) is primarily constructed through photographs and film footage from the era, a partial, plastic, monochrome version of history infiltrates not just the way we remember the past, but also the way we feel about it. As Spielberg himself notes, 'Virtually everything I've seen on the Holocaust is in black and white, so my vision of the Holocaust is what I've seen in documentaries and in books, which have largely been stark black and white images.'[13]

While the bleak contrasts of monochrome and the bleached-out shades of slightly lit colour evoke the horrors of the past for Spielberg as a director, diffuse light can also be used to communicate a character's experience of remembrance, so that the light and colour of the film image fluctuates in line with the intensity of a protagonist's shifting feelings and recollections. In this context films speak the inner lives of their characters through the language of illumination. In *A Single Man* (Tom Ford, 2009) partially saturated flat lighting strips the image of colour evoking the desolate feelings of recently bereaved George Falconer (Colin Firth) as much as it reflects the uncertainty of memory and the glamour of the past. Although blown-out light is effectively an excess of on-screen illumination, here it looks like less, since it causes the edges of objects and people to appear hazy and indistinct, as though they are slowly merging with their surroundings. Walking around his modern 1960s apartment in a starched white shirt and dark tie at the start of the film, George seems to blend in with the wooden objects and glass surfaces of the world around him. His skin is milky, lightly tan; almost grey like the flecks in his hair. He seems to be slowly disappearing into the browns, creams and whites of the 1960s past he inhabits, merging with the mahogany dashboard of his 1958 Mercedes, as though he exists in a subdued state of purgatory between the real world and the death by suicide he spends most of the film planning. George's muted almost monochromatic existence reflects the austere repression of his own feelings, as he mourns the loss of his partner in an era that is unready to believe in the validity of homosexual love. The lonely numbness of loss is communicated through the softness of illumination, as though George were living life through the frozen misty-grey eyes of his dead lover Jim (Matthew Goode) who George dreams of kissing on the snowy roadside. As George says at the start of the film, 'For the first time in my life I can't see my future. Every day goes by in a haze.'

At key moments in the film, however, George's own memories and fantasies overwhelm the screen in madeleine waves of brightly saturated illumination. On campus at the university where he teaches English, as George enjoys the soft curve of a receptionist's red lips, in close-up they bloom with intense colour. Similarly, walking near the tennis courts with a colleague, the bare chests of the racquet-wielding young

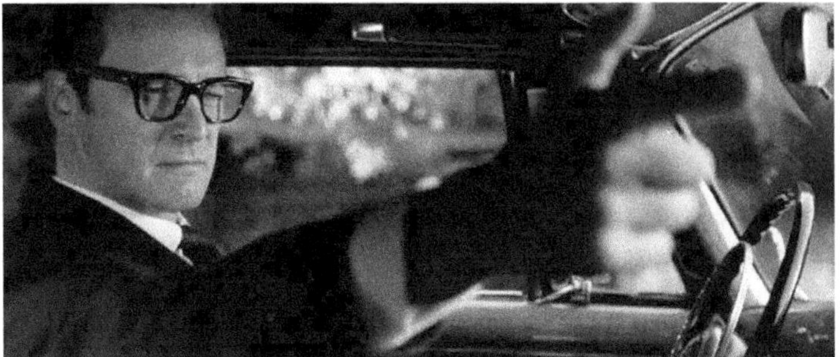

25 *A Single Man.* George's (Colin Firth) desolation mutes the colour of his experience

men draw George's eye, before bursting out of the screen in glistening, rippling, honey-tanned slow motion. As the film progresses, George grows close to one of his students, Kenny (Nicholas Hoult), whom he imagines in brightly lit, extreme colour every time they meet. Indeed, shifting light and colour communicates the way that all of George's passions, from the men he is attracted to, to laughing with his best friend Charlie (Julianne Moore) to the smell of the Jack Russell who died in the car alongside Jim are far more vivid than his almost-monochrome everyday life. The jarring juxtaposition between George's stultifying present existence and his vibrant fantasy life ensures that we feel the absence of the bright life George has lost more acutely. During one moment of remembrance, however, George's experience of the past mirrors that of the cinema. In the bank, clearing out his safety deposit box, he comes across a black-and-white photograph of Jim naked. The image triggers a tender high-contrast monochrome memory. The pastel tones of the 1960s past filter through a second level of remembrance, emerging on the other side in graphic shades of light and dark. At the end of the film, after George realises through Kenny that a love of the small pleasures in life might offer a return to high-colour existence, under the strange light of a smoggy orange moon he decides not to kill himself and locks away his gun. Sitting on the edge of his bed, contemplating his decision, he is suddenly wracked by the intense pain of a heart attack. As George's life leaves him on his bedroom floor, the colour drains from the image too, returning the frame to monochrome before a white-out signals his departure from the world. Throughout, the film remembers the piercing anguish of lost love, the intense vibrancy of fantasy and the imagined filmic glamour of the 1960s past through shifting tones of muted light and colour.

Thinking the past in colour

As with the black-and-white image, when the past is represented with intense illumination and full-colour, cine-photographic history is plundered for its somewhat 'artificial' tones and hues in order to differentiate this reconstructed image from the more technologically advanced 'realistic' colour of the present. Of course, the specific kinds of colour that have become associated with the past shift apace with new technological development, so that it is possible to distinguish different photographic and cinematic periods from the quality of the film stock used. The light and shade captured with Autochrome is different from Dufaycolor, which again differs from Kodachrome and Technicolor. Each modification in film stock or processing technique resulted in a shift in the texture of the light and colour in the frame, making it possible to differentiate between eras in the present day via the texture and tone of the cinematography. In this way, contemporary films are able to plunder photographic and cinematic history in order to appropriate the atmosphere of a specific time period. Films that do this can be simultaneously and somewhat paradoxically visualised as both more artificial *and* more naturalised since just like the monochrome contemporary film, they do not reference the actual past, but rather a pre-made, photo-filmic, coloured reconstruction of the past.

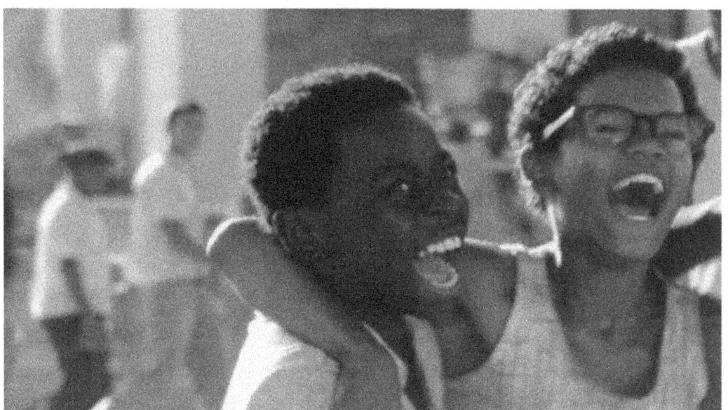

26 *City of God/Cidade de Deus.* Yellow tones and orange light warm Li'l Dice (Leandro Firmino) and Bené (Michel de Souza), evoking the heat of the favela and suggesting that the past was a safer place

City of God (*Cidade de Deus*, Fernando Meirelles, 2002) uses subtle shifts in the quality of its light via filters and film stock to mark the film's passage of time across three decades. In the section set in the 1960s warm tones of yellow and orange light evoke not only the heat of the favela, but also a nostalgic sense that the past was in some way safer than the present, since this part of the film (apart from the bloody rampage of a young Li'l Zé (Leandro Firmino)), depicts opportunistic acts of violent crime, as opposed to the organised gang warfare of later years. Certain colours seem in some way aligned to specific periods of the past, as though through its similarity to the sepia tones of a decomposing photograph, this yellow hue presents a more evocative version, and perhaps even a more accurate and direct recollection of the 1960s as it has been remembered in images. As the film shifts into the 1970s, and the level of violence within the film increases in line with Li'l Zé's power-hungry ascent and Rocket's (Alexandre Rodriguez) progression to maturity, it switches colour tone, so that whereas before the characters were bathed in forgiving, positive, warm hues of gold, now they are visualised through a variety of bright and garish shades. At this point in the film the hellish consequences of Li'l Zé's rise to power are coming to fruition, implying that colder, brighter tones are thus seemingly less nostalgic, more associated with the harsh reality of murder in the favella, than with an idealised less violent past. In the final section of the film, in which Li'l Zé is hunted by the police and eventually killed by the next generation of increasingly violent and lawless infant drug dealers, colour in the film seems to drain away, in a reflection of 'the mood at this point [which] is cold, tense and monochromatic'.[14] In this way, light and colour in *City of God* shifts in accordance with both time period and emotion, suggesting a subtle connection between hue, memory and realism of the kind Daniel Frampton highlights here: 'A film may think its colours historically – in Sally Potter's *Orlando*, as the film moves through different ages, so the film thinks these times according to their cinematic style, moving from soft romantic periods to sharp modern images.'[15]

Todd Haynes's film *Far from Heaven* (2002) engages more overtly in the replication of the coloured cinematic past through its strong lighting and colour palette that directly quotes the films of Douglas Sirk (especially *All that Heaven Allows* (1955) and *Written on the Wind* (1956)) in its transference of intense feeling from the repressed internal experiences of its heroine Cathy Whitaker (Julianne Moore) onto the surface of the image. Cathy lives a normal 1950s suburban life until she walks in on her husband Frank (Dennis Quaid) kissing a man in his office. The devastation of this revelation alienates Cathy from all that she held to be true and pushes her into a taboo friendship with her black gardener Raymond (Dennis Haybert). As the friendship blossoms into love, the pressures of 1950s society stack up against the couple, so that Raymond and Cathy must remain apart, unable to fulfil their romantic desire for one another. In a reflection of Cathy and Raymond's doomed romance, the film's *mise-en-scène* is imbued throughout with a sense of the natural beauty of death, since, until its final scene, the characters seem to inhabit a perpetually autumnal world in which the last orange flush of natural colour constantly burns upon the leaves of the trees.

Haynes uses coloured filters and lights in most of the scenes inside the family home, so that the couple's sadness and sense of entrapment seems to be refracted out of their bodies and into the blue and green light that surrounds them whenever they are 'indoors'. The dim light during these moments echoes the dark secrecy of Frank's sexuality, while the moody blue colour scheme suggests that his intense emotions will not remain buried for long. Later in the film Frank's anger erupts and he hits Kathy in the same midnight-blue front room. Inky darkness conceals domestic violence. At the same time, Cathy's sumptuous 1950s costumes that swish around her heels in plumes of orange, red, brown and purple, work in counterpoint to the lighting so that instead of a specific colour matching a specific mood (blue for sadness, red for anger for example), Haynes creates a complex system of emotive tones that can both complement and clash, soothe and enrage, suggesting a more realistic experience of emotional colour alignment in which a suppressed cacophony of feeling pushes out of the body and necessarily results in a multi-toned overload of on-screen illumination. The film works as a citation of Douglas Sirk's opulent work from the 1950s, transposing themes of societal pressure, emotional repression, forbidden love and familial unrest onto a contemporary film that emphasises its own intention to seek out, reimagine and remember the 1950s. In this way *Far from Heaven* seems to be nostalgic for a time when colourful cinematic decadence and the foregrounding of 'women's issues' combined to produce a kind of visual emotional power that spectators could recognise, empathise with and use to unravel their own emotional problems. As Pam Cook suggests:

> The activity of pastiche is foregrounded, and used to full effect as the film-makers lovingly reconstruct the Sirk

'look' through set design, costume and cinematography, and meticulously reproduce the image of 1950s small-town America projected by those melodramas. This results in a compelling emotional appeal to audiences via memories of those films, which were themselves calculated to produce a powerful affective response in viewers ... The result is an intensification of nostalgia, as the sense of loss engendered by Sirk films is doubled by that produced by their reconstruction.[16]

Cook's analysis of the systems of identification and remembrance operating in the film works against many of the assumed conventions of pastiche in which the reconstruction of a past form in a contemporary environment results in a loss, as opposed to a doubling, of emotional nostalgic attachment to the image. Cook attributes this increased sense of emotive alignment in the film to the subtle, nuanced performances of the actors, and the way in which Haynes directs as if wholly immersed in his genre, suggesting that in order for a filmic reconstruction to avoid parody, the actors, filmmakers and spectators alike must study images and emotions from the past before representing them in the present. Unlike the black-and-white films discussed previously that seem to directly reference the photographic past through their monochrome presentation of serious historical events, *Far from Heaven* remembers its past emotionally and filmically, not as historical reality but as mediated through the brightly coloured moving image and its evocation of an intense level of feeling. In its representation of a cinematic imaginary, *Far from Heaven* reflects Daniel Frampton's discussion of *Malcolm X* (Spike Lee, 1992) and *Goodfellas* (Martin Scorsese, 1990) with regard to the way in which all these films portray the filmic uncertainty of remembrance. 'Both [*Malcolm X* and *Goodfellas*] are a thinking through history with colour images, *a thinking that takes its concept from cinema's history*'.[17]

When reconstructing images of the past (in colour) in the present, filmmakers self-reflexively seek to replicate, not the

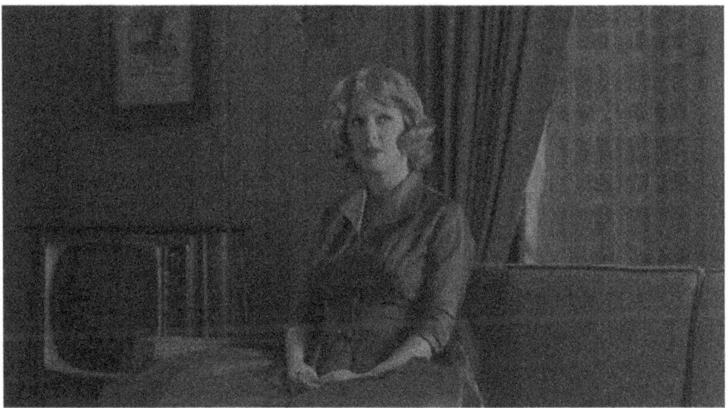

27 *Far from Heaven*. Cathy's (Julianne Moore) suppressed emotions flood the screen with moody-blue colour

colour and light of the world as it was, but rather, the world as it was recorded photo-cinematically: the light of past eras as it was captured on the celluloid strips of past films. These films construct and authenticate their histories as much through the replication of the coloured stylistic tropes of the cinematic past as through monochromatic photographic nostalgia. Through manipulations in colour stock, filters and lighting, contemporary films set in the past seek to reuse cinematic history itself in order to summon up the dominant emotional drive of a specific era for the nostalgic spectator, conjuring a filmic, plastic past that aims to intensify emotive spectatorship. What emerges is a multilayered, intertextual system of referencing and remembering history via lighting techniques that are imbued with familiar photo-filmic styles through which the past is filtered and eventually reconstructed. This idea reinforces the concept of a light-infused photographically defined notion of history that dominates and overwhelms the construction of cultural memory.

Notes

1 See J. Aumont's discussion of the temporal function of all images in which he distinguishes between the dual temporalities of observation and image as '*l'image dans le temps*' (the image in time) and '*le temps de l'image*' (the time of the image), in *l'Image* (Paris: Éditions Nathan, 1990), pp. 121–3.

2 See R. Bacon, *Opus Majus* (1267), ed., with intro and analytical table by J. H. Bridges (London: Williams and Norgate, 1900); I. Newton, *Opticks: A Treatise of the Inflections, Refractions, Inflections and Colours of Light* (London: Sam Smith and Benjamin Walford, 1704); J. W. von Goethe, *Theory of Colours* (1840), trans. Charles Lock Eastlake (London: Frank Cass, 1967).

3 See L. Hughes, 'No longer in the eye of the beholder', *Guardian* (4 September 1990), p. 7; R. Mathews, 'When Seeing Is Not Believing', *New Scientist* (October 1993), pp. 13–15; W. J. Mitchell, *The Reconfigured Eye: Visual Truth in the Post-Photographic Era* (Cambridge, MA: MIT Press, 1992).

4 See S. Sontag, *On Photography* (London: Penguin, 1977/2002), pp. 140–1; R. Barthes: 'color is a coating applied *later on* to the original truth of the black and white photograph. For me, color is an artifice, a cosmetic (like the kind used to paint corpses)' (*Camera Lucida* (London: Vintage, 1980/2000), p. 81).

5 P. Cook, 'Rethinking Nostalgia: *In the Mood for Love* and *Far from Heaven*', in P. Cook, *Screening the Past: Memory and Nostalgia in Cinema* (London and New York: Routledge, 2005), pp. 1–22, 3. A. Kuhn similarly defines nostalgia as 'a very specific type of memory: nostalgia, a bittersweet longing for a lost or otherwise unattainable object' (*An Everyday Magic: Cinema and Cultural Memory* (London: Tauris, 2002), p. 212).

6 See Cook, 'Rethinking Nostalgia'; C. Lury, *Prosthetic Culture: Photography, Memory, Identity* (London and New York: Routledge, 1998), p. 3.

7 See G. Fuller, '*The Good German*', review, *Sight & Sound*, 17(3) (March 2007), 58–60, 60; A. Taubin, '"Degraded Dupes": Steven Soderbergh', *Sight & Sound*, 17(3) (March 2007), 26–9, 28.

8 See G. Andrew, 'The Revenge of the Children', interview with

Michael Haneke, *Sight & Sound*, 19(12) (December 2009), 14–17, 17.

 9 *Ibid.*
10 See A. Wood, 'Pixel Visions: Digital Intermediates and Micromanipulations of the Image', *Film Criticism*, 32(1) (Fall 2007), 72–94, 72.
11 Lury, *Prosthetic Culture*, p. 3. Lury cites D. Ihde, 'Image Technologies and Traditional Culture', in A. Feenberg and A. Hannay (eds), *Technology and the Politics of Knowledge* (Bloomington and Indianapolis: Indiana University Press, 1995), pp. 147–59.
12 S. Spielberg in Franciszek Palowski, *Witness: The Making of Schindler's List* (London: Orion, 1998) p. 112.
13 S. Spielberg, *Schindler's List*, DVD box information (Universal Studios and Amblin Entertainment, 1993).
14 J. Oppenheimer, 'Boys from Brazil', *American Cinematographer*, 84(2) (February 2003), 83–90, 83–4.
15 Frampton, *Filmosophy*, p. 120.
16 Cook, 'Rethinking Nostalgia', p. 12.
17 D. Frampton, 'Colour', in *New Scholarship from BFI Research* (London: BFI, 1995), pp. 100–1.

6   The magic hour

Immersed in the gloaming, it is here that we are brought potentially into the contemplation of our own existence.

(Martin Barnes, *The Gloaming*)[1]

In the half-light your skin glowed with life.

(Lidia (Jeanne Moreau) reading Giovanni's (Marcello Mastroianni) words in *La notte*)

As the sun sits below the horizon and the world darkens or brightens at dusk or dawn, natural illumination enters an uncanny twilight stage between existence and oblivion. In this luminous interstitial half-light, blue shadows and lyrical lighting effects encourage thoughtful, intriguing introspection and intense, restless experiences. As a result, ever since photographic equipment became fast enough to harness some of twilight's subtleties, both photographers and cinematographers have been consistently drawn to its elegiac fades, to the unusual spectacle of its temporal, visual and emotional possibilities. Due to its fleeting, iridescent nature, twilight is difficult to faithfully capture and record, presenting those who wish to film it with an alluring technical challenge, since these magical lighting effects are constantly in flux, existing partially in ephemeral states for brief periods of time.

Accordingly, twilight cannot be described as a single tone or intensity of light. It continually evolves, warming the verdant earth with pastel shades at dawn, receding towards murky inscrutability at dusk, encompassing technicolour crepuscular rays, pale grey-white skies and midnight-blue hues between the official gloaming hours of civil, nautical and astronomical twilight as the sun wavers at 6, 12 and 18 degrees below the horizon. Multiple names reflect twilight's shifting, poetic nature: dusk, dawn, nightfall, daybreak, half-light, afterglow, the gloaming. And then there are the special twilight 'hours': the golden hour, the violet hour, the blue hour, the magic hour, each describing a particular colour, quality or experience of interstitial illumination. Constantly transitioning in shade and strength, twilight runs through a cinematographer's grasp like sand in an upturned hourglass, and yet it is this very elusive intangibility that makes it a desirable, evocative and memorable cinematic experience. Like the cinema itself, twilight oscillates between darkness and illumination.

It is, of course, the emotional weight of twilight that filmmakers are most drawn to. The immediacy of twilight's atmospheric allusions combined with its shifting uncertainty and the difficulties associated with its record, make it a valuable tool to represent explorations of the soul, while offering the chance for cinema to reveal the breadth of its lavish visual potential. In films as seemingly diverse as *La notte* (*The Night*, Michelangelo Antonioni, 1961), *The Birds* (Alfred Hitchcock, 1963) and *Donnie Darko* (Richard Kelly, 2001), in monochrome greys or moody blues, twilight is used to amplify notions of disenchantment, desire, uncanny horror and encroaching insanity. As light glimmers or dims and shifts its shape, transforming familiar environments into glowing blue-grey landscapes, settings and locations become shrouded in mystery, pregnant with narrative potential, while characters retreat within, wandering alone, anxious or confused, contemplating the strange amorphous worlds around them. Twilight's uncanny atmosphere is due to its intangible nature. At this time of day it is difficult to tell in an instant whether illumination is departing or returning, whether characters are heading towards danger or are about to be saved. This tension gives rise to strange, uneasy sensations. Normality has reached a tipping point. Everything that was certain becomes unsure, the recognisable becomes indistinct, mountain ranges become black shadows, blue seas turn silvery grey. Amidst these visceral, charged atmospheres, characters do not feel or seem themselves, they struggle with psychological disruptions, with issues of alienation, loneliness and abandonment, while consistently contemplating existential questions regarding the nature and purpose of life itself.

Twilight isn't just an uncanny feature of natural illumination to be swiftly and skilfully captured by conscientious filmmakers outdoors. At night in the modern world our lives are dominated by electric lights that lend a twilit sheen to everything we do after dark. The dim yellow flicker of candles and firelight has evolved into the phosphorus neon buzz of filaments and bulbs, strip lights and streetlights, monitors and screens. Technology prolongs twilight states long after the sun has set. True darkness is rarely experienced. Instead, constructed half-light has become increasingly familiar. Similarly, the feelings, sensations and visual quality of the gloaming infiltrate innumerable films in relative shades, intensities and atmospheres. As this book has explored, a diverse range of filmmakers have harnessed twilight's evocative interstitial qualities either naturally or artificially. The uncertain shifting identities of Colonel Kurtz and Harry Lime in *Apocalypse Now* and *The Third Man* are mapped in fleeting moments of golden light against inky darkness where revelation and inscrutability collide. Christian vanishes amidst the midnight hues of natural twilight, tied to a tree in a forest in *The Celebration*, as his family attempt to stifle the claims of abuse he desperately tries to bring to light. Two versions of the imaginary are brought to life via electric twilight shades in *Blade Runner* and *Three Colours: Blue*. In the former Deckerd operates in a fluorescent dystopic future half-light, while in the latter, Julie experiences bitter-sweet musical memories in violent violet waves. Mysterious shadows mark transitional twilight states and terrifying replicated souls in *Nosferatu*, while in *Far from Heaven*'s constructed Sirkian past Kathy silently implodes, rallying between duty and devotion amidst the stifling indigo shades of her claustrophobic domestic interior.

Across all these films, twilight marks more than just a time of day. Over and above any other instance or quality of illumination, twilight exudes emotive potency, directly connecting characters to specific environments during distinct moments in time. The visuals, atmospheres and emotions associated with the gloaming seem to penetrate both the psychic spaces of the characters and the films' narrative concerns, dominating the surface and substance of cinema itself. Because they glow, at times all films look and feel like twilight. Indeed a twilight aesthetic has become directly associated with cinema as a medium. 'Cinematic' photographers including Gregory Crewdson, Nan Goldin, Bill Henson and Phillip Lorca diCorcia, are often identified as such, not just because of the size and scale of their images, or because of their production methods, but because of their pregnant displays of dreamy, laconic characters amidst gloomy, glowing twilight settings. Twilight draws attention to cinema's own ontology since it is situated at the intersection of practical illumination (content) and expressive feeling (style). It is for this reason that this chapter is the last in this book – twilight is film light at its most essential, encompassing all the forms and functions that film light has demonstrated so far: a focus on the interiority of identity, the spectacle of authentic illumination, the fantasy spaces of the imaginary, the mysteries and myths of the dark, and the uncertain interstitial fading light of the past. As a site and a moment of captivating visual revelations and transitions, the cinematic encounter can itself be considered a threshold experience akin to twilight, since the sensation of sitting immersed in darkness, while a beam of light projects luminous moving images that partially illuminate glowing faces, recalls the heightened emotive space of the magic hour, where the spectator is caught between illumination and darkness, between the dream on-screen and waking life.

The black-and-white blue hour

As much as twilight is a moment in time and a quality of light, it is also a feeling and an impulse, an uncanny atmosphere detectable across monochrome as well as colour cinema. Since twilight is best recognised by its opulent visual displays of unusual colours, in monochrome cinema it is more difficult to detect, seeping across the screen in various pale-grey tones. Without twilight's dramatic colour shifts, black-and-white cinema relies on subtle lighting transitions to communicate those intense emotional moments that take place at dusk or dawn. A car's headlights shining brightly while the land remains illuminated, the flicker of a streetlight against a pallid sky, characters in contemplative moods as they wake or prepare to sleep: each clue marks a twilight time of day, and with it a sense of transition, introspection and drama. In black-and-white cinema twilight is the mid-point of the fade, the greyness around the borders of every monochrome image, the colour of shadows. Like the characters that move through it, the gloaming hints at darkness while clinging to the light.

Two films made in Italy in the early 1960s use moments of twilight to emphasise their monochrome narratives of hedonism, alienation and emotional apocalypse. *La Dolce Vita* (Federico Fellini, 1960) is full of multiple, decadent dawns. After sleeping together for the first time, Marcello (Marcello Mastroianni) and Madellena (Anouk Aimée) leave the prostitute's house where they've been staying at daybreak. They drive past new housing blocks in the early morning light: the tiny illuminated bulbs outside each window working as the only visual indication of the time of day. Later, in his own shiny sports car, Marcello speeds down the road towards his flat. Although the sky is brighter, his headlights are switched

on and the landscape remains shrouded in gloom: a dimness
that anticipates his despair when he returns home and realises
his fiancée Emma has taken an overdose. A few days later
when Marcello interviews Sylvia (Anita Ekberg), a beautiful
Hollywood movie star, he stays out late into the night drinking
and dancing with her. After she has a row with her boyfriend
Robert, Marcello takes her for a drive in his sports car. Together
they wander the streets of Rome until she bathes in the Trevi
Fountain. As Marcello approaches, in awe of her beauty, they
embrace and the fountain stops flowing. The sudden silence
startles, marking a shift in mood, as the film cuts to a wide
shot, and the even grey light (along with a bicyclist in the
foreground on his way to work) indicates that morning has
broken. When Marcello drops Sylvia off outside her flat she says
good morning to her angry boyfriend Robert and goodnight to
Marcello. Her choice of words marks both the interstitial time
of day and her wavering state of mind.

Half-way through the film, the use of twilight shifts from
explanatory nocturnal decadence to expressive instants of
danger, death and resurrection. In a nearby town, two local
children claim they can communicate with the Madonna.
Marcello goes with Emma and a cameraman to investigate.
A large crowd gathers in the evening to receive a blessing. As
dusk recedes into night, it begins to rain and the celebrated
children run around the field shouting that they can see the
Madonna, causing the crowd to stampede. In the ensuing
chaos a man dies. Shrouded in the magical cold light of dawn,
Marcello and Emma watch in anguish as he is laid to rest on
holy ground. The half-light notes their subdued manner as
much as it marks the transition of a soul from one state to the
next. Later, Marcello's father comes to visit, and after a night of
heavy drinking with his son he accompanies a French dancing
girl back to her flat. Marcello is about to leave them when the
girl tells him that his father has fallen ill. He finds his father
sitting, watching the dawn break over the city. Twilight shades
make palpable Marcello's sense that his father will not be with

him for long so that when his father voices his wish to return home, Marcello begs him to stay. Multiple drunken, delirious dawns follow. Each one draws attention to twilight's secondary definition as something or someone who operates outside ordinary society, who exists or functions beyond the laws and morals of everyday life. At the end of the film, Marcello attends one final party after he finds out his friend Steiner has committed suicide, taking his two children with him. For the first time, as everyone dances, Marcello loses control. He gets drunk and covers the room in feathers until the guests stagger and skip, bleary-eyed, through pine trees towards the sea at daybreak. As they walk, one of the guests voices the connection between twilight and emotion in the film when he says to Marcello, 'Ahhh Nature! Dawn always has such an effect on me.' At the end of the sequence, as the light begins to grow on the beach, Marcello sees a young girl he previously called an angel. He waves at her and they try to communicate above the sound of the surf with hand signals. Finally, in the brightening light, she watches him leave the beach, smiling directly into the camera, and through it, into cinematic space. Her fresh young face in the dawn light underscores the decadence of Marcello's previous twilights while hinting at his potential salvation.

In Antonioni's *La notte*, twilight marks a similar transitional, revelatory phase in the lives of its main characters. Instead of multiple dawns, however, *La notte* focuses on a single night, the afternoon preceding it, and the evocative moments of dusk and daybreak in between. Giovanni (again played by Marcello Mastroianni) and Lidia (Jeanne Moreau) have been married for ten years. At the start of the film they visit their friend Tommaso who is dying in hospital. The sight of their friend's pain and the realisation that he will soon be dead forces the couple to examine their own feelings for one another, and to react in different ways to the notion of their own mortality. Giovanni consoles and distracts himself with a series of romantic encounters with other women. Although similar opportunities for infidelity present themselves, Lidia rejects all advances and instead retreats inside herself, wandering through streets and parties alone, encountering violence and decay. As the sun sets behind diffuse clouds, Lidia leaves a party that is being held to celebrate Giovanni's novel and takes a taxi to the outskirts of the city. In the waning light she comes across a gang of men fighting. At first she retreats, but as the sound of their punches grows louder, she runs towards them and screams at them to stop. One of the fighters does as she asks before following Lidia as she runs around the corner. It is unclear if he wishes to do her harm, or wants to talk. As she approaches her taxi, the screen darkens incrementally and streetlights once again glow in the pale sky. The uncertain light reflects the hesitant atmosphere, caught somewhere between menace and sensuality.

In almost every scene twilight infuses the atmosphere of *La notte*'s settings and reflects the emotions of its protagonists. At home in the gloom, unsure of Lidia's whereabouts, Giovanni waits for her to return. As the light leaves their apartment, it seems to exist in shades of grey like their distant, undefined relationship, lacking the stark graphic lines of definitive black and white. In this environment, Giovanni's suited body begins to merge with his surroundings: his faded shirt and skin echo the pale tones of the sky outside, while his charcoal suit and tie reflect the architectural lines and deep shadows of the moody interiors. While Lidia waits for Giovanni to pick her up in a field near where they used to live, she contemplatively watches the silver crepuscular rays of the sun shining their last from behind a cloud. After dusk, back at home, Giovanni's disinterested gaze incites Lidia's decision to go out. At first they drink and dine alone in a bar, but, again, Lidia becomes restless and they leave for a millionaire's party outside the city. At the party Lidia telephones the hospital and discovers that Tommaso has died. She is devastated but keeps the news to herself. Giovanni becomes close to Valentina (Monica Vitti), a girl that Lidia has marked out for her husband in an almost

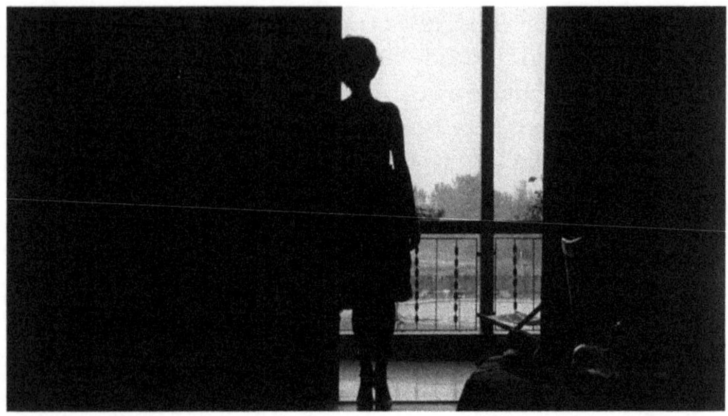

28   *The Night/La notte.* Valentina (Monica Vitti) greets the dawn with the curves of her silhouette

identical dress. When Lidia returns towards the end of the night after rejecting the advances of a male friend during a rain storm, she meets Giovanni in Valentina's room. After discussing the night's events in a detached, civilised manner, Valentina stands with her back to the window, saying goodbye to the couple, revealing the dawn with the curves of her soft outline moulded against the pale light outside. As Lidia and Giovanni leave, the lights in the room go out, leaving Valentina alone and iconic as a black silhouette against a softening sky. Outside Lidia and Giovanni wander through the golf course on the grounds in the growing light. They sit by a sand bunker and Lidia reveals to a distraught Giovanni that Tommaso is dead. The hitherto unspoken tensions of their relationship unravel as the light intensifies. Lidia reads a letter full of love and understanding that Giovanni has forgotten he wrote to her. She cries, aware that their love has gone and they desperately embrace. Throughout the film, the shifting interstitial light that surrounds both the couple and the night echoes the indeterminate status of their relationship as well as an encroaching sense of the inevitability of death: a promise that swirls just out of reach in the grey half-light of their lost romance. It is in the filmic light of these twilight greys that 1960s European art-house cinema, so key to cinema's sense of its modern self, finds its existentialism, its fascination with death and its own self-referentiality.

Always dying, never dead

In full colour, twilight cinema is at once more recognisable, more arresting and more uncertain. As well as the shifting tones of twilight, colour film also records the hues of the magic hour in transition, evolving from golden sunsets through purple hazes and blue shadows towards the electric-green half-light of mottled night. When subdued rainbow shades diffuse across the sky of the screen, bleeding into one another before receding, cinematic aesthetics reach an apex of visual intensity and emotional force. These poetic moments of luminous expression are used to mark the beauty and horror of both the natural world and human nature, while emphasising uncanny primal fears and fractured liminal states.

Reminiscing about his mother's death, on a beach just after sundown, gazing across the dappled blues and greys of the sea, stones and sky in *The Thin Red Line* (Terrence Malick, 1998) in voice-over Private Witt (James Caviezel) considers his mortality: 'I wondered how it would be when I died, what it would be like to know that this breath now was the last one you was ever gonna draw. I just hope I can meet it the same way she did, with the same calm. Cause that's where it's hidden: the immortality I've seen.' The end of a day provokes consideration of the end of life, just as Private Bell's (Benjamin Chapman) deep-blue fantasies of the wife he has left at home infuse the screen with melancholy nostalgia and love. This sense of quiet contemplation, framed with notions of existence, transience and faith pervades all Malick's scenes at twilight in this Second World War epic, including those tinged with suspense that occur before and after battles amidst the green rushes of the lush ridge where so many men meet their end. Like the films of Godard, de Sica, Richardson and Vinterberg discussed in Chapter 2, Malick embraces natural illumination and its propensity to add genuine feeling to the frame. Even at moments of great stress, twilight's raw beauty provokes comment. On the line to Captain James Staros (Elias Koteas), Lieutenant Colonel Gordon Tall (Nick Nolte) describes the early morning light with a reference to Homer's goddess of the dawn 'Eos rhododactylos: rosy-fingered dawn', before ordering him to send his men to fight. The pale-red sky he describes proves fitting since during the course of the day on the ridge blood seeps into the grass and almost all the men lose their lives.

Later, crouching on the ridge in soft-blue twilight, 1st Sergeant Edward Welsh (Sean Penn) wonders at what it is that sets Private Witt apart from all the other men. He questions why he always puts others before himself while remaining so calm in the line of fire. Welsh asks, 'What difference do you think you can make, one single man in all this madness. If you die it's gonna be for nothing. There's not some other world out there where everything's gonna be ok. There's just this one, just this rock.' Private Witt doesn't reply. Instead he stares at Welsh with a serene look on his face before gazing towards the heavens at the moon and the palms in the darkening sky as an answer. Many times in *The Thin Red Line*, Malick's camera turns skyward, watching the shifting rays through the trees, finding lyricism in nature, anticipating the luminous authentic light work he would do with sunrises and sunsets and notions of the afterlife in *The New World* (2005) and *Tree of Life* (2011). References to sparks of life and golden rays are profuse in Malick's cinema, constantly grounding characters in the magnificence of natural surroundings, reaffirming the beauty of simple things. At twilight in these charged atmospheres, light reveals its glorious potential. Magical shifting light evokes the passage of time, its wax and wane is literally visible on the

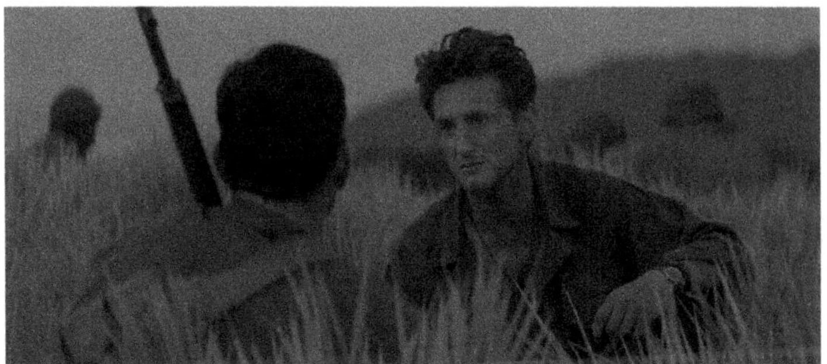

29 *The Thin Red Line*. Sergeant Edward Walsh (Sean Penn) and Private Witt (James Caviezel) discuss the meaning of life at twilight

screen, in turn evoking the transience of life. With the swirling constellation of light at the start and end of *Tree of Life*, Malick suggests that light is God, and that since light is at its most wondrous and atmospheric at twilight, it is during this fleeting time of day that cinematic illumination is also at its most spiritual. Malick's cinema epitomises a key impulse in contemporary cinema: unrelentingly visual, where the qualities of luxurious light and lush cinematography have become strong selling points, from Michael Mann to Steven Soderbergh to Lynne Ramsay. This is (twi)light as fetish – the influence of European art cinema means there is an attempt at the existential, but now the representation, the visual experience of the light, has become as important as those emotions which it purports to represent.

There is a point, however, as twilight dips towards the night, that its natural beauty becomes strange, uncomfortable and distinctly abnormal. During this part of the magic hour, contemplation slips towards fantasy, while primal fears rise with the proximity of the night. In the cinema, this potent moment is marked by science-fiction notions of the 'twilight zone' and by the accordant terrors of dusk and respites of dawn that mark the vampire film genre. As recent titles attest, from *Near Dark* (Kathryn Bigelow, 1987) to *From Dusk till Dawn* (Robert Rodriguez, 1996) and *Twilight* (Catherine Hardwicke, 2008), a vampire's undead half-life is most evocatively portrayed in half-light. When twilight occurs during unusual times of day, as it does at the end of *The Eclipse* (*L'Eclisse*, Michelangelo Antonioni, 1962) during an eclipse, or, simply because the early-morning sun has disappeared behind clouds, as depicted in the closing moments of *The Birds* (Alfred Hitchcock, 1963) it embodies an uncanny atmosphere. In these scenes, just like the everyday rooks and seagulls gathered on wires against the purple dawn skies, waiting to attack in Hitchcock's film, horror often arises when the everyday becomes aberrant.

Part of the strangeness of the closing moments of *The Birds* is due to the stunning visual texture of the light in its final composite shot and to the optical printing techniques used. Hitchcock said that this was 'the most difficult single shot [he had] ever done'.[2] As the car containing Mitch, Lydia, Kathy and an injured Melanie creeps down the track away from the house, in the foreground scores of birds have gathered in vast flocks, consuming the screen with their feathers, wings and beaks. A few vibrant rays from the just-risen sun gleam from behind the clouds, glinting off the car as it makes its escape down the bird-strewn road, transforming the space with eerie blue-grey twilight. The shot, initially created by Albert Whitlock using matte painting techniques, required hundreds of dummies and live birds as well as thirty-two different exposures overseen by animator and photographic expert Ub Iwerks, before Hitchcock achieved the specific tones and shades of light that would communicate the conflicting magic hour emotions of anxiety, ambiguity and relief he desired.[3] The astounding technical complexity of this final shot and Hitchcock's determination to achieve the twilight effects that transform the frame, prefigures the use of CGI digital techniques in the 1990s that began to mould and shape everyday illumination into evocative half-light shades with relative ease.

Two films that straddle the millennium embody twilight's uncertainty, depicting protagonists who may or may not be dead, while exemplifying the way lighting techniques (especially in coloured twilight hues) began to be recreated by CGI. *Donnie Darko* is marked by its digitally enhanced inky colours that recall the tonal and technical complexities of the finals scenes of *The Birds*, replicating those moments after sunset or before dawn when the birds sing eerily in the trees and when light has either almost gone out or is about to illuminate the world. Set in 1980s suburban America, the film follows imaginative, troubled teenager Donnie Darko (Jake Gyllenhaal) during the final twenty-eight days, six hours, forty-two minutes and twelve seconds before he thinks the world is going to end. Like the twilight world he inhabits, Donnie is trapped in a liminal state: caught not just in the transitional period of adolescence, but also between the reality of the outside world and the fantasies inside his head, between the illumination of existence and the darkness of oblivion.

Twilight acts as a visual gateway in the film, defining a near fantasy space that uses the mid-point between darkness and illumination to symbolise Donnie's mental journey from his exterior conscious environment into his inner subconscious world. The film begins at dawn. While the sound of morning birdsong and faraway thunder play quietly on the soundtrack, the camera tracks down a Californian road towards Donnie who is lying in the street, his bike strewn to one side, just waking up from another sleepwalking episode. As he stirs and gets up, the camera pulls out to share in the beautiful view of misty-blue hills, the trees in the foreground like violet silhouettes waiting to be touched by the light. This moment of Donnie's awakening anticipates the film that will follow: the dawn light gives the scene an unnerving, magical atmosphere that is at once beautiful and strange. In the cinema, this kind of low lighting is expressive and evocative: the screen obtains a radiant sheen that conjures mythical and mental allusions. Here, then, twilight provides its own spatio-temporal connections,

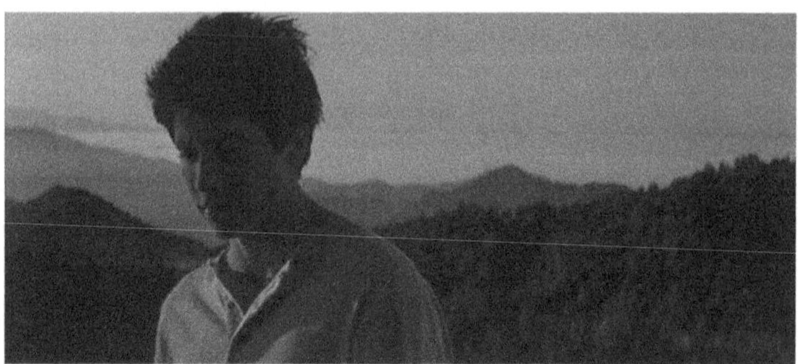

30   *Donnie Darko*. Donnie (Jake Gyllenhaal) wakes from
sleepwalking in the hills in the uncanny dawn light

operating as a threshold, indicating links between the moments
when Donnie is asleep and awake, questioning the reality of
his conscious world, and working as a direct indication of key
moments of psychological revelation and insight.[4]

Aesthetically more synthetic than *Donnie Darko*, David
Fincher's *Fight Club* (1999) is set in an artificial green-blue
twilight, a layered dystopian darkness illuminated by electric
light within which the film's unnamed protagonist (Edward
Norton) also descends ever deeper into the depths of his
psyche. *Fight Club* uses computer-generated twilight to literally
visualise the space of its protagonists' mind on film. The
title sequence begins inside the protagonist's brain. Amidst
a swirling, gloomy half-light, the titles glow and explode as
the camera eddies through electrified neural pathways until
it pulls out of his head in three-dimensional CGI layers, past
skin pores and hair dripping with sweat, up the gleaming
metal shaft of a gun that charismatic anarchist Tyler Durden
(Brad Pitt) is thrusting into the protagonist's mouth. It is soon
revealed that this opening is a flash-forward to the film's final
scenes. Durden has kidnapped the protagonist and is holding
him on the top floor of a building that is about to be blown
up by the demolitions committee of 'Project Mayhem'. The

eerie twilight in which the protagonist sits, directly recalls the environment of his brain since it glows and throbs with a similar murky green light and is punctuated by flashes of electric luminosity from the twenty-four-hour city around him. Lustrous digital lights and multiple screens create the twilight of the city, depicting an uncertain world of thresholds in which neither daylight nor total darkness exists.

It is electric twilight that similarly transforms on-screen space and embodies the protagonist's inner mental turmoil in *Donnie Darko*. At midnight Donnie sleepwalks. A voice calls to him from outside and he gets out of bed to look for its source. In the garden a man in a rabbit suit called Frank tells Donnie that the world is about to end. At this time of night, constructed lighting converts darkness into the colours of the gloaming. Glowing bedside lamps, chandeliers and dim streetlamps transform Donnie's safe, suburban reality into a mythical, uncertain world where space atrophies, enabling only close-up, intimate interactions during which a lack of strong lighting encourages the spectator to question the validity of the events on-screen. While all the moments in the film during which Donnie sleepwalks in a semi-conscious state are indicated through the use of this kind of natural or electric twilight, it is interesting to note that the scenes in which he talks to his psychiatrist in her office are also shot with low-level lights. This retreat into a semi-darkened room in which Donnie's deepest hopes and fears are explored works to visually suggest a shift into his unconscious mind, as though in near-darkness investigations of the soul can be more easily and effectively undertaken. The dim light of the psychiatrist's office directly links the twilight events of Donnie's unconscious mind to his exploration of those events in waking hours, suggesting a more fluid relationship between the scenes in which he is awake and those when he is asleep.

Fight Club's protagonist is also going slowly insane. By day he has a mind-numbing job working as a recall coordinator for a leading car manufacturer; by night, the monotonous materialist grind has given him severe insomnia that is only alleviated by his regular visits to self-help groups where he gets therapy for illnesses he doesn't have. His life is transformed when he meets Durden on a plane, and the two attempt to regain their masculinity by setting up illegal underground fight clubs in which the emasculated men of the city congregate to beat each other until they feel alive. At the self-help group for men with testicular cancer, like Donnie's psychiatrist's office, the room is dim, its lack of light working to tone down and shrink the space in an attempt to create a comfortable setting in which these men can relax and share their private fears. At the same time, however, the condensed light makes the men appear lost and isolated, their white faces illuminated in a twilight that implies both a loss of identity and a slightly comic obsession with the self.

Underground in the Fight Club, again, the lighting is muted, apparently illuminated by a series of low-wattage bulbs overhead. Through word of mouth, the event has become increasingly popular, so that in the electric twilight numerous men now take it in turns to beat each other to a pulp. As Amy Taubin has evocatively described, 'shot in a wet-dream half-light that gilds the men's bodies as they pound each other's heads into the cement, the Fight Club sequences are such a perfect balance of aesthetics and adrenalin they feel like a solution to the mind/body split'.[5] When combined with emotive, luminous lighting, it is once again liquid, in this case in the form of sweat and blood, and its reflective qualities that gives the screen a kind of poetic resonance, lending these images of men destroying bodies an electric sheen of radiant beauty.

In Durden's house on Paper Street the two men live in self-inflicted twilight. By day the windows remain boarded up, by night they are unable to electrify the house because every time it rains it floods, threatening electrocution. Instead they light the house with candles, so that space shrinks and eerie yellow-green light pervades the screen. Once again, the house can be read as a constructed representation of the protagonist's deteriorating state of mind. Not only is the roof leaking, but there are also holes in the floor and the pipes don't work. When, towards the end of the film, it is revealed in a final shocking twist that in fact the protagonist *is* Durden, that Pitt's character is in fact an imaginary product of the protagonist's psychotic mind, the dystopian twilight of the house on the aptly named Paper Street in which Pitt's character has digitally constructed sex in one room while the protagonist listens in another, resonates even more intensely as a symbol of his fractured mental state and split personality. Almost every tone or intensity of light in *Fight Club* evokes the interstitiality of the magic hour. From the greeny-blue CGI lighting inside the protagonist's brain, to the dim interiors of the self-help groups, to the seeping dystopic colour wash, and the tinged candlelight, to the electric twilight of the protagonist's final view of total destruction. During the film's final moments, after the protagonist has rid himself of Durden by shooting himself in the mouth, he stands with his girlfriend Marla at the top of the skyscraper he was in at the start of the film, waiting for the buildings to explode. As the detonators go off, the couple turn towards the huge glass windows, holding hands in the magical blue twilight, watching in awe as the glowing lights in the computer-generated buildings are extinguished and one by one they fall to the ground. In this scene, light is transformed from a natural phenomenon to a human-made event. Even more than in the mechanical, electric past, in this early digital era of CGI, light is no longer a direct referent of reality. Instead it has become a transformative atmospheric tool, a malleable vehicle through which the emotional drive of a film can be viscerally reconstructed and communicated in synthetic twilight shades. As the lights go out on each of the buildings outside the window, the couple are left in an even gloomier twilight, standing together holding hands in the gloaming, like a modern-day Adam and Eve, once more waiting for the world to light up and begin again.

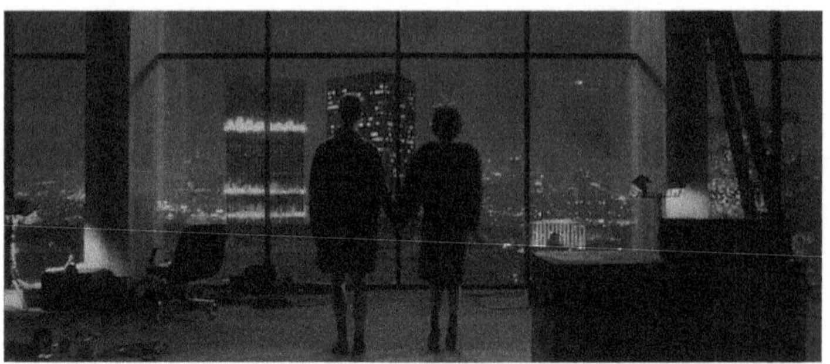

31   *Fight Club*. The unnamed protagonist (Edward Norton) and
Marla (Helena Bonham-Carter) watch hand in hand as the city
is destroyed and electric twilight dims

At the end of *Donnie Darko* it is revealed that for almost
its entire length, Donnie has been dead, killed while asleep
in his bed, by the falling engine of a jet plane that travelled
through a portal in space and time. Thus almost the entire
film can be read as a representation of Donnie's death state,
transforming him into a kind of spectre or ghost who is
attempting to unravel the meaning of his life. Caught on
the brink between life and death, Donnie and Tyler Durden
become like the photograms embedded in the substance of
cinema, those rectangular photographic frames, flickering in
the twilight, hidden from reality, but present nevertheless. At
the same time, as much as they reflect the photogram, they
also recalls Roland Barthes's concept of the photograph. They
are spectres of the real, deathly images of their former selves, at
once dead and going to die. They are also, of course, fictional
apparitions, characters with no referent to the real, and as such
they confirm Barthes's concept of the cinema as a medium,
which, like these characters, 'does not make a claim in favour
of its reality'.[6]
In both these films twilight demarcates a liminal
space between forms of being. The protagonists and their
environments exist in a transitory position where states of

presence and absence, reality and fantasy, waking and sleeping, sanity and madness, illumination and darkness coalesce. Their indefinable, intermediate positions highlight an uncertainty that dogs all film characters. Since twilight is a magical time when the dying or rising sun plays tricks with illumination, at the far reaches of the visual spectrum, like Pitt's character in *Fight Club* and Donnie in *Donnie Darko*, it can also represent the possibility of not being fully illuminated, of not being able to be captured on film, of not existing at all. In comparison to the strident studio lighting that falls on Falconetti's face in *La passion de Jeanne d'Arc*, or Monroe's in *Gentlemen Prefer Blondes*, constructing faces so well lit it seems almost impossible to question their existence, at twilight it is difficult to tell whether the sun is falling or rising, whether life is over or yet to begin, and, in the cinema at least, whether that light or the lives of those it falls on ever existed at all. *Fight Club* and *Donnie Darko* remind us that although their protagonists stand partially illuminated before our eyes, not only do they potentially not exist within their filmic narratives, like all characters across the history of cinema, they also do not exist outside of the filmic glow. They are constructed with light and nothing else. As surely as day transitions through the gloaming into night, they will be wiped away when the credits roll and we walk out of the cinema into the bright world beyond.

Notes

1 M. Barnes, 'The Gloaming', in M. Barnes and K. Best (eds), *Twilight: Photography in the Magic Hour* (London and New York: Merrell, 2006), pp. 10–23, p. 22. Published to accompany an exhibition of the same name that took place at the Victoria & Albert Museum, London, 11 October–17 December 2006. The exhibition included work by Robert Adams, Gregory Crewdson, Ori Gersht, Bill Henson, Chrystel Lebas, Philip-Lorca diCorcia, Liang Yue and Boris Mikhailov.

2 See P. McGilligan, *Alfred Hitchcock: A Life in Darkness and Light* (Chichester and New York: Wiley and HarperCollins, 2003), pp. 628–9.
3 *Ibid.*
4 It is interesting to note that according to Sharon Packer in 2007, *Donnie Darko* was the film most cited by male psychiatric patients as inducing episodes of stress and unease. As Packer explains, 'Films can also induce anxiety, because they tap into realistic or unrealistic fears about the past, present, or future. It is not uncommon for patients to call a psychiatrist claiming that their sleep problems or panic attacks began after seeing a specific film. In the author's experience, *Donnie Darko* (2001) holds the record for inducing male anxiety. This cult film … was uncannily similar to the airplane attack on the World Trade Center, so much so that it was pulled from theatres soon after its initial release in 2001' (*Movies and the Modern Psyche* (Westport: Praeger, 2007), p. 4).
5 A. Taubin, 'So Good It Hurts', *Sight & Sound*, 9(11) (November 1999), 16–18, 17–18.
6 Barthes, *Camera Lucida*, p. 89.

Afterglow

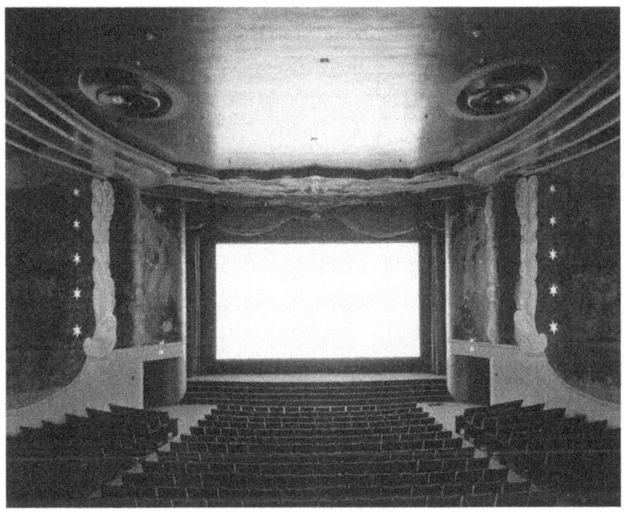

32 Hollywood Cinerama, LA, 2003. Hiroshi Sugimoto *Theatres* series

Sometimes I probably do mourn the fact that I no longer make films. This is natural and it passes. Most of all I miss working with Sven Nykvist, perhaps because we are both utterly captivated by the problems of light, the gentle, dangerous, dreamlike, living, dead, clear, misty, hot, violent, bare, sudden, dark, spring-like, falling, straight, slanting, sensual, subdued, limited, poisonous, calming, pale light.

(Ingmar Bergman, *Magic Lantern: An Autobiography*, 1988)

In the cinema, as in life, light appears infinitely malleable and meaningful. As a tool of expression it presents the filmmaker with seemingly unlimited avenues for textural creativity and emotive exposition. And yet, as this book has aimed to highlight, for all its connotative elasticity, its suggestive, boundless variety, on-screen, light's uses and affects, its meaning and emotion *do* follow recognisable patterns and traditions: luminous, familiar visual codes that wax and wane from film noir to digital animation across the spectrum of film history. Identities are constructed and identification enabled with striking eye lights and delayed strongly lit close-ups that push us ever closer to our star infatuations. An unavoidable or self-imposed absence of artificial illumination encourages creative use of architectural structures and arresting, rarefied natural effects that transform everyday light into spectacular screen experiences. Abundant electric and computer-generated light connotes the modern, the fantastic and the futuristic, authenticating robotic, android and alien bodies while moulding cinematic space into the bursts and glimmers of interior emotional representation. Shadows and dark spaces evoke mythic solidity and catalyse primal fears, while receding memories of both the actual and the reconstructed past edge out of sight in muted, insubstantial, barely-there shades. Finally, the screen world harnesses the uncanny subjective sensations of the gloaming, borrowing its interstitial glow and evocative temporal fluctuations to suggest and amplify crucial transitional moments in the lives of philosophising characters hovering in near-death dream states.

While light in film is used variously and particularly within the diegesis of these stories and styles, the light that comes from the screen itself – cinema's ever-present afterglow – binds together all these cinematic experiences. As the architecture of cinematic space shifts backwards and forwards from theatres to front rooms, from widescreen to 3D, from computers to hand-held devices, each screen continues to illuminate, while preferred viewing conditions maintain an element of darkness. Whether we experience the screen communally in blacked-out rooms or in isolated instants from the palm of our hand, it is the filmic glow – the cinematic gloaming – that consistently attracts and holds our gaze, enticing attention.

The cinema has always been sensitive to the breadth of its own intense luminous power. Half-way through *Donnie Darko*, as Donnie becomes increasingly unstable he takes his girlfriend to see *The Evil Dead* (Sam Raimi, 1981) at his local cinema. Sitting in the darkness, his face moodily glowing from the light reflecting off the cinema screen, the environment of the theatre – the colour and quality of its light – replicates almost exactly Donnie's unconscious experiences. Indeed, in these moments the interstitial combination of darkness and light that we experience in the theatre encourages a similarly contemplative, absorbing and internalised period to that which occurs during twilight hours. Films are screened in dimly lit environments that emphasise the glowing lustre of their surfaces, and yet, we never actually watch them in total darkness, since the light that shines from the films themselves creates its own glimmering conditions. In this way, the illuminated cinema experience itself can be read as a kind of threshold, a borderline, a liminal state: a twilit gap across which notions of private contemplation and collective entertainment, individual desire, ephemerality and shared spectacle unravel.

Some of the most arresting cinematic moments occur amidst the constructed glow of auditoriums on the screen, in cinemas within cinemas. When film records itself, when characters watch films in darkened theatres or view home movies indoors, our own feelings of anticipation, excitement, spectacle and contemplation are replicated on their faces in dappled twilight tones. Light reflects. Like the colours of the gloaming, the cinema mirrors itself in shifting emotional hues at crucial narrative moments. In *Breathless* and *Twelve Monkeys* (aka *12 Monkeys*, Terry Gilliam, 1995) it figures itself as a safe haven, a dim alternative space away from danger in which characters momentarily hide. In *Cinema Paradiso* (*Nuovo Cinema Paradiso*, Giuseppe Tornatore, 1988) and *True Romance* (Tony Scott, 1993), it is a magical, flickering place to fall in love. In *Rebecca, Sunset Boulevard* (Billy Wilder, 1950), *Donnie Darko* and *Fight Club*, its twilit boundaries question the border between sanity and madness, while at the beginning of *Persona* (Ingmar Bergman, 1966) and at the end of *Inglorious Basterds* (Quentin Tarantino, 2009), the appearance of a luminous face on a screen within the diegesis marks both the splitting of the self and an immortal suggestion: an ephemeral route towards life after death. In all of these deeply expressive, self-reflexive cinematic moments, amidst the magical twilight of the cinematic hour, characters are bathed in the fluctuating light of the screen, as we are before them, enveloped in cascading mechanical illumination and framed by darkness; at once constructed by, experiencing and creating light itself.

These cherished *mise-en-abyme* film moments remind us that cinematic luminosity is different to any other kind of illumination.[1] Film light is at once substance and message, thought and action, vehicle and feeling. It is both functional and emotional, encapsulating time and movement. It is not a filmmaker, but the photographer Hiroshi Sugimoto, who has most evocatively captured the sensation and spectacle of film light. Sugimoto's photographs depict various cinema theatres and their screens from the ornate to the ordinary, and are claimed to have been taken using an exposure time that lasted the entire length of a single film, creating vast white rectangles of light that illuminate dark interior spaces. His 'whole film' images encapsulate cinema's lyrical play of illumination and shadow, its drive to construct, transform and connote, capturing and condensing film light as a simultaneous spectacle of ontology and emotion. As Giuliana Bruno explains, the photographs

> 'expose' the zero degree of cinema: the transient moment
> of its emergence and passing. In his movie theatres series,

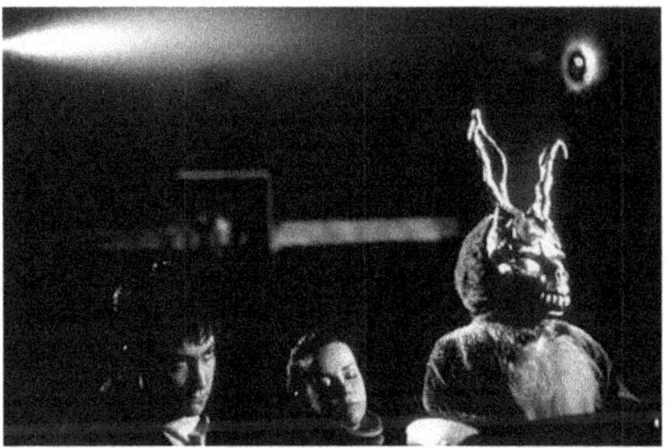

33   *Donnie Darko*. Donnie (Jake Gyllenhaal) and Gretchen (Jena Malone) watch *The Evil Dead* with Frank (James Duvall) in the Twilit Cinema

only the white film screen is made visible. Film, that is, is rendered as a geography of light.[2]

This book has attempted to map film as such a geography of light, to ask what film light is and does, to focus not on the socio-political or the historical, but on how the way a scene, shot or gesture is lit can make us think and feel. It is in the geography of Sugimoto's images that the essence of our experience of film light is unravelled. The searing white rectangle at the centre of each photograph, the film as image, recalls the definite qualities of those spotlights, streetlights and sunbeams discussed in Part I of this book, those modes of filmic illumination that embody presence, that create a solid spectacle of existence within the world whether 'real' or imagined. It is, however, in the forgotten sections of these images, in the areas around the edges of Sugimoto's screens that film light, its meaning and emotion, is fully revealed. It is those empty cinema seats, tinged by the light of the screen, languishing in shadow, hinting at occupation, that complicate notions of illumination and identity. The absence of direct light in these shadow spaces, like the chapters in Part II of this book, create an area in the image in which existence is less certain, architecturally embodying the mystery and myths of cinematic enjoyment, occupying an interstitial state of fluid identity and a pungent nostalgia for an eternally unreachable past. Together, the bright screen and the dark seats, the image and the space, *is* cinema.

This book is an invitation to re-watch iconic films with illumination in mind, to see film light afresh, to notice and reflect upon the way light in the cinema transforms and manipulates. It calls for film critics, historians and cinephiles to pay as much attention to light's emotive, meaningful powers as they have always done with motion and time, with set design and framing, with actors and directors, and as they have only recently begun to do with colour. Film light glints in the corners of every cinematic conversation and as such it should be as abundant, essential and arresting on the page as it has always been on the screen.

Notes

1 Loosely translated the term *mise-en-abyme* means 'placed into an abyss', referring to the infinite replication that occurs when two mirrors face each other. In art history and in particular in film studies, the phrase is used to indicate a self-referential duplication of images within images or scenes within scenes. In this context I have used the term to imply a kind of 'Russian doll' cinematic experience during which the spectator watches a film in which the characters are themselves watching other characters in films, a technique that doubles, reflects and references the cinematic experience.
2 G. Bruno, *Atlas of Emotion: Journeys in Art, Architecture, and Film* (New York: Verso, 2002) p. 52

Filmography

2001: A Space Odyssey. Dir. Stanley Kubrick. Metro-Goldwyn-
    Mayer/Stanley Kubrick Productions. USA 1968
Aliens. Dir. James Cameron. Twentieth Century Fox Film Corp-
    oration/Brandywine Productions/SLM Production Group.
    USA 1986
All That Heaven Allows. Dir. Douglas Sirk. Universal International
    Pictures. USA 1955
American in Paris, An. Dir. Vincente Minnelli. Loew's. USA 1951
Apocalypse Now. Dir. Francis Ford Coppola. Zoetrope Studios.
    USA 1979
Avatar. Dir. James Cameron. Twentieth Century Fox/Dune
    Enter-
    tainment/Ingenious Film Partners/Lightstorm Entertainment.
    USA/UK 2009
Basic Instinct. Dir. Paul Verhoeven. Carolco Pictures/Canal+
    USA/France 1992
Batman Begins. Dir. Christopher Nolan. Warner Bros. Pictures/
    Syncopy/DC Comics/Legendary Pictures. USA 2005
Bicycle Thieves/Ladri di biciclette. Dir. Vittorio De Sica. Produzioni
    De Sica. Italy 1948
Bigger Than Life. Dir. Nicholas Ray. Twentieth Century Fox Film
    Corporation. USA 1956
Big Sleep, The. Dir. Howard Hawks. Warner Bros. Pictures. USA
    1946
Birds, The. Dir. Alfred Hitchcock. Universal Pictures/Alfred
    J. Hitchcock Productions. USA 1963

Blade Runner. Dir. Ridley Scott. Ladd Company/Shaw Brothers/
    Warner Bros. Pictures/Michael Deeley Production/Ridley
    Scott Productions. USA, 1982

Blair Witch Project, The. Dir. Daniel Myrick and Eduardo Sánchez.
    Haxan Films. USA 1999

Blonde Venus. Dir. Josef von Sternberg. Paramount Pictures. USA
    1932

Blue Velvet. Dir. David Lynch. De Laurentiis Entertainment
    Group. USA 1986

Breathless/À bout de souffle. Dir. Jean-Luc Godard. Les
    Productions Georges de Beauregard/Société Nouvelle de
    Cinématographie. France 1960

Butch Cassidy and the Sundance Kid. Dir. George Roy Hill.
    Campanile Productions. USA 1969

Cabinet of Dr. Caligari, The/Das Cabinet des Dr. Caligari. Dir.
    Robert Weine. Decla-Bioscop AG. Germany 1920

Celebration, The/Festen. Dir. Thomas Vinterberg. Nimbus Film
    Productions/Danmarks Radio/Nordisk Film/SVT Drama.
    Denmark 1998

Cinema Paradiso/Nuovo Cinema Paradiso. Dir. Giuseppe Tornatore.
    Cristaldifilm/Les Films Ariane/Rai Tre Radiotelevisione
    Italiana/TF1 Films Production/Forum Picture. Italy 1988

City of God/Cidade de Deus. Dir. Fernando Meirelles. O2 Filmes/
    VideoFilm/Globo Filmes/Lereby Productions/Studio Canal/
    Wild Bunch. Brazil/France 2002

Close Encounters of the Third Kind. Dir. Steven Spielberg. Columbia
    Pictures Corporation/EMI Films/Julia Phillips and Michael
    Phillips Productions. USA 1977

Dark Corner, The. Dir. Henry Hathaway. Twentieth Century Fox
    Film Corporation. USA 1946

Dolce Vita, La. Dir. Federico Fellini. Riama Film/Gray-Film/
    Pathé Consortium Cinéma. Italy 1960

Donnie Darko. Dir. Richard Kelly. Pandora Films/Flower Films/
    Adam Fields Productions/Gaylord Films/Newmarket Films.
    USA 2001

Double Indemnity. Dir. Billy Wilder. Paramount Pictures. USA 1944

Eclipse, The/L'eclisse. Dir. Michelangelo Antonioni. Cineriz/
Interopa Film/Paris Film. Italy 1962

E.T. the Extra-Terrestrial. Dir. Steven Spielberg. Universal Pictures/
Amblin Entertainment. USA 1982

Eternal Sunshine of the Spotless Mind. Dir. Michel Gondry.
Anonymous Content/Focus Features/This Is That Productions.
USA 2004

Evil Dead, The. Dir. Sam Raimi. Renaissance Pictures. USA 1981

Far from Heaven. Dir. Todd Haynes. Focus Features/Vulcan
Production/Killer Films/John Wells Production/Section
Eight/Clear Blue Sky Productions/TF1 International/USA
Films. USA/France 2002

Fight Club. Dir. David Fincher. Art Linson Productions/Fox 2000
Pictures/Regency Enterprises/Taurus Film. USA/Germany
1999

Fog, The. Dir. John Carpenter. AVCO Embassy Pictures/EDI/
Debra Hill Productions. USA 1980

From Dusk till Dawn. Dir. Robert Rodriguez. Dimension Films/A
Band Apart/Los Hooligans Productions/Miramax Films.
USA 1996

Gentlemen Prefer Blondes. Dir. Howard Hawks. Twentieth Century
Fox Film Corporation. USA 1953

Goodfellas. Dir. Martin Scorsese. Warner Bros. USA 1990

Halloween. Dir. John Carpenter. Compass International Pictures/
Falcon International Productions. USA 1978

In the Mood for Love/Fa yeung nin wa. Dir. Wong Kar-wai. Block
2 Pictures/Jet Tone Production/Paradis Films. Hong Kong/
France 2000

Inglorious Basterds. Dir. Quentin Tarantino. Universal Pictures/
Weinstein Company/A Band Apart/Zehnte Babelsberg/
Visiona Romantica. USA 2009

Insomnia. Dir. Christopher Nolan. Alcon Entertainment/Witt/
Thomas Productions/Section Eight/Insomnia Productions/
Summit Entertainment. USA/Canada 2002

Landscape in the Mist/Topio stin omichli. Dir. Theodoros
Angelopoulos. Basic Cinematographica/Rai Due/Greek

Television ET-1/Compagnie Générale d'Images/Paradis
Films/Theo Angelopoulos OE/La Sept/Greek Film Center/
Sofinergie 1. Greece 1988

Malcolm X. Dir. Spike Lee. 40 Acres & A Mule Filmworks/JVC
Entertainment/Largo International NV. USA 1992

Maltese Falcon, The. Dir. John Huston. Warner Bros. Pictures.
USA 1941

Man Who Wasn't There, The. Dir. Joel and Ethan Coen. Good
Machine/Gramercy Pictures (I)/Mike Zoss Productions/KL
Line/Working Title Films. USA/UK 2001

Matrix, The. Dir. Wachowski brothers. Groucho II Film
Partnership/Silver Pictures/Village Roadshow Pictures/
Warner Bros. Pictures. USA/Australia 1999

Metropolis. Dir. Fritz Lang. Universum Film (UFA). Germany 1927

Morvern Callar. Dir. Lynne Ramsay. Company Pictures. UK 2002

Near Dark. Dir. Kathryn Bigelow. F/M/Near Dark Joint Venture.
USA 1987

New World, The. Dir. Terrence Malick. New Line Cinema/
Sunflower Productions/Sarah Green Film/First Foot Films/
Virginia Company LLC. USA 2005

Night, The/Notte, La. Dir. Michelangelo Antonioni. Nepi Film/
Silver Films/Sofitedip. Italy 1961

Night of the Hunter, The. Dir. Charles Laughton. Paul Gregory
Productions. USA 1955

Nosferatu/Nosferatu, eine Symphonie des Grauens. Dir. F. W. Murnau.
Jofa-Atalier Berlin–Johannisthal/Prana-Film GmbH.
Germany 1922

Once Upon a Time in the West/C'era una volt ail West. Dir. Sergio
Leone. Finanzia San Marco/Rafran Cinematografica/
Paramount Pictures. Italy/USA 1968

Passion of Joan of Arc, The/La passion de Jeanne d'Arc. Dir. Carl
Theodor Dreyer. Société générale des films. France 1928

Persona. Dir. Ingmar Bergman. Svensk Filmindustri. Sweden
1966

Point Blank. Dir. John Boorman. Metro-Goldwyn-Mayer. USA
1967

Raging Bull. Dir. Martin Scorsese. Chartoff–Winkler Productions. USA 1980

Rear Window. Dir. Alfred Hitchcock. Paramount Pictures/Patron Inc. USA 1954

Rebecca. Dir. Alfred Hitchcock. Selznick International Pictures. USA 1940

Saving Private Ryan. Dir. Steven Spielberg. DreamWorks SKG/Paramount Pictures/Amblin Entertainment/Mutual Film Company/Mark Gordon Productions. USA 1998

Schindler's List. Dir. Steven Spielberg. Universal Pictures/Amblin Entertainment. USA 1993

Searchers, The. Dir. John Ford. Warner Bros. Pictures/C. V. Whitney Pictures. USA 1956

Sin City. Dir. Robert Rodriguez and Frank Miller. Dimension Films/Troublemaker Studios. USA 2005

Single Man, A. Dir. Tom Ford. Fade to Black Productions/Depth of Field/Artina Films. USA 2009

Social Network, The. Dir. David Fincher. Columbia Pictures/Relativity Media/Scott Rudin Productions/Michael De Luca Productions/Trigger Street Productions. USA 2010

Star Wars. Dir. George Lucas. Lucasfilm/Twentieth Century Fox Film Corporation. USA 1977

Stranger, The. Dir. Orson Welles. International Pictures/Haig Corporation. USA 1946

Sunset Boulevard. Dir. Billy Wilder. Paramount Pictures. USA 1950

Sunshine. Dir. Danny Boyle. DNA Films/Fox Searchlight Pictures/Ingenious Film Partners/Moving Picture Company/UK Film Council. UK/USA 2007

Taste of Honey, A. Dir. Tony Richardson. Woodfall Film Productions. UK 1961

Terminator, The. Dir. James Cameron. Hemdale Film/Pacific Western/Euro Film Funding/Cinema 84. USA 1984

Thin Red Line, The. Dir. Terrence Malick. Fox 2000 Pictures/Geisler-Roberdeau/Phoenix Pictures. USA 1998

Third Man, The. Dir. Carol Reed. London Film Productions/British Lion Film Corporation. UK 1949

Three Colours: Blue/Trois couleurs: bleu. Dir. Krzysztof Kieslowski. Canal+/Conseil de l'Europe/CAB Productions/CED Productions/Eurimages/France 3 Cinéma/MK2 Productions/Zespol Filmowy 'Tor'. France/Poland/Switzerland 1993

Touch of Evil. Dir. Orson Welles. Universal International Pictures. USA 1958

Tree of Life, The. Dir. Terrence Malick. Brace Cove Productions/Cottonwood Pictures/Plan B Entertainment/River Road Entertainment. USA 2011

Trip to the Moon, A/Le voyage dans la lune. Dir. Georges Méliès. Star-Film. France 1902

TRON: Legacy. Dir. Joseph Kosinski. Walt Disney Pictures/Sean Bailey Productions/LivePlanet. USA 2010

True Romance. Dir. Tony Scott. Morgan Creek Productions/Davis-Films/August Entertainment. USA/France 1993

Twelve Monkeys. Dir. Terry Gilliam. Universal Pictures/Atlas Entertainment/Classico. USA 1995

Twilight. Dir. Catherine Hardwicke. Summit Entertainment/Temple Hill Entertainment/Maverick Films/Imprint Entertainment/Goldcrest Pictures/Twilight Productions. USA 2008

Vertigo. Dir. Alfred Hitchcock. Alfred J. Hitchcock Productions. USA 1958

WALL.E. Dir. Andrew Stanton. Walt Disney Pictures/Pixar Animation Studios. USA 2008

War of the Worlds. Dir. Byron Haskin. Paramount Pictures. USA 1953

War of the Worlds. Dir. Steven Spielberg. Paramount Pictures/DreamWorks SKG/Amblin Entertainment/Cruise/Wagner Productions. USA 2005

White Ribbon, The/Das Weiße Band. Dir. Michael Haneke. XFilme Creative Pool/Wega Film/Les Films du Losange/Lucky Red. Germany/Austria/France/Italy 2009

Written on the Wind. Dir. Douglas Sirk. Universal International Pictures. USA 1956

Bibliography

Alton, John, *Painting with Light* (London and New York: Routledge, 1997)

Andrew, Geoff, 'The Revenge of the Children', interview with Michael Haneke, *Sight & Sound*, 19(12) (December 2009)

Anker, Roy M., *Catching Light: Looking for God in the Movies* (Michigan and Cambridge: Eerdmans, 2004)

Arnheim, Rudolph, *Film as Art* (London: University of California Press, 1933/57)

Aumont, Jacques (ed), *Aesthetics of Film*, with Alain Bergala, Michel Marie, Marc Vernet (trans. Richard Neupert) (Austin: University of Texas Press, 1983/92)

— *L'image* (Paris: Editions Nathan, 1990)

— *L'attrait de la lumière* (Crisnée: Éditions Yellow Now, 2010)

Bacon, Roger, *Opus Majus* (1267) (ed), with intro and analytical table by J. H. Bridges (London: Williams and Norgate, 1900)

Barnes, Martin, 'The Gloaming', in M. Barnes and K. Best, *Twilight: Photography in the Magic Hour* (London and New York: Merrell, 2006)

Barthes, Roland, *Camera Lucida* (London: Vintage, 1980/2000)

Baxandall, Michael, *Shadows and Enlightenment* (New Haven and London: Yale University Press, 1995)

Baxter, Peter, 'On the History and Ideology of Film Lighting', *Screen*, 16(3) (1975), 83–106

Bordwell, David, *The Films of Carl-Theodor Dreyer* (Berkeley, Los Angeles and London: University of California Press, 1981)

— and Kristin Thompson, *Film Art: An Introduction (7th Edition)* (New York: McGraw-Hill, 2004)

Bould, Mark, *Film Noir: From Berlin to Sin City* (London and New York: Wallflower, 2005)

Bruno, Giuliana, *Atlas of Emotion: Journeys in Art, Architecture and Film* (New York: Verso, 2002)

Budge, E. A. Wallis, *The Egyptian Book of the Dead (The Papyrus of Ani)* (New York: Dover, 1969)

Bukatman, Scott, 'The Artificial Infinite: On Special Effects and the Sublime', in Annette Kuhn (ed), *Alien Zone II: The Spaces of Science Fiction Cinema* (London and New York: Verso, 1999), pp. 249–75

Chion, Michel, *Kubrick's Cinema Odyssey* (London: BFI, 2001)

Clarke, Arthur C., *2001: A Space Odyssey*, based on the screenplay by Arthur C. Clarke and Stanley Kubrick (London: Hutchinson, 1968)

Clover, Joshua, *The Matrix, BFI Modern Classic* (London: BFI, 2004)

Connor, Steven, 'A Certain Slant of Light', in M. Barnes and K. Best, *Twilight: Photography in the Magic Hour* (London and New York: Merrell, 2006)

Cook, Pam, *Screening the Past: Memory and Nostalgia in Cinema* (London and New York: Routledge, 2005)

— (ed), *The Cinema Book 3rd Edition* (London: BFI, 2007)

Coutard, Raoul, 'Light of Day', *Sight & Sound*, 35(1) (1966), 9–11

Dalle Vacche, Angela *Cinema and Painting: How Art Is Used in Film* (Austin: University of Texas Press, 1996)

Deleuze, Gilles, *Cinema 1: The Movement Image* (London: Athlone, 1983/86)

Dibbets, Karel and Bert Hogenkamp (eds), *Film and the First World War* (Amsterdam: Amsterdam University Press, 1995)

Dyer, Richard, 'A White Star', *Sight & Sound*, 3(8) (1993), 22–5

— *White* (London and New York: Routledge, 1997)

Eliot, C. W. (ed), *Homer (Harvard Classics)* (Danbury, CT: Grolier, 1980)

Ellison, Ralph, *Invisible Man* (London: Penguin, 1965 [first published 1952])

Elsaesser, Thomas, *Metropolis (BFI Film Classic)* (London: BFI, 2000)

Epstein, Jean, 'Magnification' (1921), in Richard Abel, *French Film Theory and Criticism: A History/Anthology 1907–1939 Vol. I* (Princeton, NJ: Princeton University Press, 1988), pp. 235–41

Factor, M., 'Standardisation of Motion Picture Make-up', *Journal of the Society of Motion Picture Engineers*, 28(1) (1937), 52–62

Farquharson, Alex, *The Magic Hour: The Convergence of Art and Las Vegas* (Ostfildern, Germany: Hatje Cantz Verlag, 2001)

Fisher, David J., *The Craft of Film: Part III: Film Stocks* (London: Attic, 1969)

Frampton, Daniel, 'Colour' (1995) in Colin McCabe and Duncan Petrie (eds), *New Scholarship from BFI Research* (London: BFI, 1995)

— *Filmosophy* (London: Wallflower, 2006)

Fuller, Graeme, '*The Good German*', review, *Sight & Sound*, 17(3) (March 2007), 58–60

Goethe, J. W. von, *Theory of Colours*, trans. Charles Lock Eastlake (London: Frank Cass [1840] 1967)

Gombrich, E. H., *Shadows: The Depiction of Cast Shadows in Western Art* (London: National Gallery, 1995) [companion to the exhibition]

Grainge, Paul, *Memory and Popular Film* (Manchester and New York: Manchester University Press, 2003)

Gunning, Tom 'Lunar Illuminations', in J. Geiger and R. L. Rutsky (eds), *Film Analysis: A Norton Reader* (New York and London: Norton, 2005), pp. 64–81

Halley, J. and P. Ticineto Clough, *The Affective Turn: Theorizing the Social* (Durham, NC: Duke University Press, 2007)

Haltof, Marek, *The Cinema of Krzysztof Kieslowski: Variations on Destiny and Chance* (London: Wallflower, 2004)

Higham, Charles and Joel Greenberg, '*Noir* Cinema' (1968), in Alain Silver and James Ursini (eds), *Film Noir Reader* (New York: Limelight, 1996) pp. 27–36

Higson, Andrew, 'Space, Place, Spectacle: Landscape and Townscape in the "Kitchen Sink" Film', in Andrew Higson (ed), *Dissolving Views: Key Writings on British Cinema* (London: Cassell, 1996), pp. 133–56

Hills, Paul, *The Light of Early Italian Painting* (London: Yale University Press, 1987)

Hughes, L., 'No longer in the eye of the beholder', *Guardian* (4 September 1990), p. 7EG

Iaccino, James F., *Psychological Reflections on Cinematic Terror* (Westport, CT and London: Praeger, 1994)

Ihde, D., 'Image Technologies and Traditional Culture', in A. Feenberg and A. Hannay (eds), *Technology and the Politics of Knowledge* (Bloomington and Indianapolis: Indiana University Press, 1995), pp. 147–59

Jacobsen, Wolfgang and Werner Sudendorf, *Metropolis: A Cinematic Laboratory for Modern Architecture* (Stuttgart and London: Edition Axel Menges, 2000)

Jones, Darryl, *Horror: A Thematic History in Fiction and Film* (London: Arnold, 2002)

Keating, Patrick, *Hollywood Lighting from the Silent Era to Film Noir* (New York: Columbia University Press, 2010)

Kelly, Richard, *The Name of this Book is Dogme 95* (London: Faber and Faber, 2000)

King, Geoff (ed), *The Spectacle of the Real: From Hollywood to Reality TV and Beyond* (Bristol and Oregon: Intellect Books, 2005)

— and Tanya Krzywinska (eds), *Science Fiction Cinema: From Outerspace to Cyberspace* (London: Wallflower, 2000)

Knox, Donald, *The Magic Factory: How MGM Made An American in Paris* (New York and London: Praeger, 1973)

Kolker, Robert (ed), *Stanley Kubrick's 2001: A Space Odyssey* (Oxford and New York: Oxford University Press, 2006)

Krauss, Rosalind, 'Tracing Nadar', *October* 5 (1978), 29–47

Kuhn, Annette, (ed), *Alien Zone II: The Spaces of Science Fiction Cinema* (London and New York: Verso, 1999)

— *An Everyday Magic: Cinema and Cultural Memory* (London: Tauris, 2002)

Landsberg, Alison, 'Prosthetic Memory: The Ethics and Politics of Memory in an Age of Mass Culture', in Paul Grainge, *Memory and Popular Film* (Manchester and New York: Manchester University Press, 2003), pp. 144–61

Lay, Samantha, *British Social Realism: From Documentary to Brit Grit* (London: Wallflower, 2002)

Lippit, Akira Mizuta, *Atomic Light (Shadow Optics)* (Minneapolis and London: University of Minnesota Press, 2005)

Lury, Celia, *Prosthetic Culture: Photography, Memory, Identity* (London and New York: Routledge, 1998)

Lynch, David K. and William Livingston, *Color and Light in Nature* (Cambridge: Cambridge University Press, 2001)

McGilligan, Patrick, *Alfred Hitchcock: A Life in Darkness and Light* (Chichester and New York: Wiley and HarperCollins, 2003)

Mathews, R., 'When Seeing Is Not Believing', *New Scientist* (October 1993), pp. 13–15

Méliès, Georges, 'Cinematographic Views' (1906), in Richard Abel, *French Film Theory and Criticism: A History/Anthology 1907–1939 Vol. I* (Princeton, NJ: Princeton University Press, 1988), pp. 35–47

Metz, Christian, *Film Language: A Semiotics of the Cinema* (New York: Oxford University Press, 1974)

Mitchell, William J., *The Reconfigured Eye: Visual Truth in the Post-Photographic Era* (Cambridge, MA: MIT Press, 1992)

Nash, Mark, 'Notes on the Dreyer Text', originally published in 1977 in Mark Nash (ed), *Screen Theory Culture* (Basingstoke and New York: Palgrave Macmillan, 2008)

Neumann, Dietrich (ed), *Film Architecture: Set Designs from Metropolis to Blade Runner* (Munich and New York: Prestel, 1996)

Newton, Isaac, *Opticks: A Treatise of the Inflections, Refractions, Inflections and Colours of Light* (London: Sam Smith and Benjamin Walford, 1704)

Oppenheimer, Jean, 'Boys from Brazil', *American Cinematographer*, 84(2) (February 2003), 83–90

O'Pray, Mike, *Film, Form and Phantasy: Adrian Stokes and Film Aesthetics* (New York: Palgrave Macmillan, 2004)

Packer, Sharon, *Movies and the Modern Psyche* (Westport: Praeger, 2007)

Palowski, Franciszek, *Witness: The Making of Schindler's List* (London: Orion, 1998)

Pavlus, John, 'Forget Me Not', *American Cinematographer*, 85(4) (April 2004), 36–47

Perkins, V. F., *Film as Film* (London: Penguin, 1972)

Place, Janey and Peterson, Lowell, 'Some Visual Motifs of *Film Noir*' (1974), in A. Silver and J. Ursini (eds), *Film Noir Reader* (New York: Limelight, 1996), pp. 65–76

Plantinga, C. and Greg M. Smith, *Passionate Views: Film, Cognition and Emotion* (Baltimore: John Hopkins University Press, 1999)

Podalsky, Laura, *The Politics of Affect and Emotion in Latin American Cinema* (New York: Palgrave Macmillan, 2011)

Powell, Anna, *Deleuze, Altered States and Film* (Edinburgh: Edinburgh University Press, 2007)

Rank, Otto, *The Double: A Psychoanalytic Study* (North Carolina: University of North Carolina Press, 1971)

Roberts, Ian *German Expressionist Cinema: The World of Light and Shadow* (London: Wallflower, 2008)

Robinson, Henry Peach, *Pictorial Effect in Photography* (London: Piper and Carter, 1869)

Rutherford, Emma, *Silhouette* (New York: Rizzoli International Publications, 2009)

Salt, Barry, *Film Style and Technology: History and Analysis* 2nd Edition (London: Starword, 1992)

Schivelbusch, Wolfgang, *Disenchanted Night: The Industrialization of Light in the Nineteenth Century* (Berkeley, Los Angeles and London: University of California Press, 1988)

Shiel, Mark, *Italian Neorealism: Rebuilding the Cinematic City* (London and New York: Wallflower, 2006)

Silver, Alain and James Ursini (eds), *Film Noir Reader* (New York: Limelight, 1996)

Smith, Murray, *Engaging Characters: Fiction, Emotion and the Cinema* (New York: Oxford University Press, 1995)

Sontag, Susan, *On Photography* (London: Penguin, 1977/2002)

Sternberg, Joseph von, 'More Light', *Sight & Sound*, 25(2) (1955–56), 70–5 and 109–10

Stoichita, Victor I., *A Short History of the Shadow* (London: Reaktion, 1997)

Stok, Danusia (ed), *Kieslowski on Kieslowski* (London and Boston: Faber and Faber, 1993)

Tan, Ed, *Emotion and the Structure of Narrative Film: Film as an Emotion Machine* (London: Routledge, 1995)

Taubin, Amy, 'So Good It Hurts', *Sight & Sound*, 9(11) (November 1999), 16–18

— '"Degraded Dupes": Steven Soderbergh', *Sight & Sound*, 17(3) (March 2007), 26–9

Thomson, Kristin, 'The International Exploration of Cinematic Expressivity', in K. Dibbets and B. Hogenkamp (eds), *Film and the First World War* (Amsterdam: Amsterdam University Press, 1995), pp. 65–85

Toles, George, *A House Made of Light: Essays on the Art of Film* (Detroit, MI: Wayne State University Press, 2001)

Turim, Maureen, *Flashbacks in Film: Memory and History* (New York and London: Routledge, 1989)

Walters, James, *Alternative Worlds in Hollywood Cinema* (Bristol and Chicago: Intellect Books, 2008)

Webber, Andrew and Emma Wilson (eds), *Cities in Transition: The Moving Image and the Modern Metropolis* (London and New York: Wallflower, 2008)

Wells, Paul, *The Horror Genre: From Beelzebub to Blair Witch* (London: Wallflower, 2000)

Willis, Holly, *New Digital Cinema: Reinventing the Moving Image* (London: Wallflower, 2005)

Wood, Alexis, 'Pixel Visions: Digital Intermediates and Micromanipulations of the Image', *Film Criticism*, 32(1) (Fall 2007), pp. 72–94

Index

Note: page numbers in italic refer to illustrations, 'n' after a page reference indicates the number of a note on that page

EU authorised representative for GPSR:
Easy Access System Europe, Mustamäe tee 50,
10621 Tallinn, Estonia
gpsr.requests@easproject.com